brilliant

start-up

brilliant

start-up
second edition

**How successful entrepreneurs set up and run a
brilliant business**

Caspian Woods

Prentice Hall
is an imprint of

Harlow, England • London • New York • Boston • San Francisco • Toronto • Sydney • Singapore • Hong Kong
Tokyo • Seoul • Taipei • New Delhi • Cape Town • Madrid • Mexico City • Amsterdam • Munich • Paris • Milan

PEARSON EDUCATION LIMITED

Edinburgh Gate
Harlow CM20 2JE
Tel: +44 (0)1279 623623
Fax: +44 (0)1279 431059
Website: www.pearson.com/uk

First published in Great Britain in 2008
Second edition published 2011

© Caspian Woods 2008, 2011

The right of Caspian Woods to be identified as author of this work has
been asserted by him in accordance with the Copyright, Designs and
Patents Act 1988.

Pearson Education is not responsible for the content of third-party internet sites.

ISBN: 978-0-273-76197-6

British Library Cataloguing-in-Publication Data
A catalogue record for this book is available from the British Library

Library of Congress Cataloging-in-Publication Data
A catalog record for this book is available from the Library of Congress

10 9 8 7 6 5 4 3 2 1
15 14 13 12 11

Typeset in 10/14pt Plantin by 30
Printed and bound in Great Britain by Henry Ling Ltd, Dorchester, Dorset

Dedicated to Scarlett and Felix, budding entrepreneurs

Contents

About the author		viii
Acknowledgements		ix
How this book works		x

phase 1 **Preparation** — 1

Step 1	Brace yourself	3
Step 2	Work on your brilliant business idea	13
Step 3	Road test your idea	35
Step 4	Build your support network	47
Step 5	Your business plan	61
Step 6	Reduce your start-up costs	67
Step 7	Raise finance	79
Step 8	Take care of the small print	99

phase 2 **Into action** — 109

Step 9	Get selling	111
Step 10	Set your price	133
Step 11	Now, make your product/service	145
Step 12	Get the cash in	155
Step 13	Do your books	163
Step 14	Do a quick risk audit	175

phase 3 **Up and running** — 181

| Step 15 | Taking on staff | 183 |
| Step 16 | Make sales easier: marketing | 195 |

Epilogue		211
Useful contacts		213
Index		217

About the author

Caspian Woods is proud never to have had a job.

As a student, he started his first business, 'Time of Your Life', as the UK's first yearbook publisher, managing to miss the Facebook phenomenon completely. He ran an events company called 'Let Me Hold Your Balls For You' and launched an e-commerce magazine by living for a week in a shop window six months before the dotcom crash.

For the past 13 years, he has worked with his team to build Editions Financial into the UK's leading financial content marketing agency, advising some of the UK's biggest banks on their communication strategies.

He is author of *From Acorns*, also from Pearson, and writes newspaper columns. Along the way, he has picked up a number of awards such as Young Achievers of Britain at Buckingham Palace, Shell LiveWIRE and the Young Scot of the Year Award (despite being neither young nor Scottish).

Acknowledgements

I'd like to herald our fantastic team at Editions Financial.

To Scarlett and Felix for inspiration, and helping me rearrange book shop displays when no-one was looking.

You must really love the business of publishing to put up with authors. So my thanks go to the team at Pearson; Elie Williams and Rachel Hayter.

And to my father for inspiring me to always try to fit more into my life.

How this book works

It's simple to start a business.

You chuck your job in. The next day, you set up with a computer in your spare room. Someone buys your product and you make a profit.

The hard part is surviving. This means overcoming the 50/50 odds of failure in your first year, and 95 per cent odds of failure by year five. It means getting to a point where you have staff doing your job better than you, or enough money to retire, or you have changed the world through what you do.

That's worth working for. And that's what this book sets out to do.

This book isn't like most other start-up guides. It's different in three ways.

It only features the essentials

There are acres of facts about start-up, so I've boiled this book down into what I believe are the essentials. You might not agree with all my advice, but at least my recommendations are crystal clear.

I've broken the book down into 3 phases:

- Phase 1: Preparation.
- Phase 2: Into action.
- Phase 3: Up and running.

Within these three phases there are 16 steps to get your business up and running.

There's no time limit to this. It might take you a year or you might rattle through it all in two weeks. That's up to you. But you do have to go through all the steps.

It's largely common sense

Business isn't rocket science. But it can help to learn the lessons of others who've been there before you. Therefore I've tried to pack this book full of real-life examples. In this second edition, I've also included some brilliant examples from around the world.

I've also highlighted the common reasons businesses fail:

- giving up
- not making enough sales
- running out of cash
- not protecting your business
- falling sick
- legal and contractual disputes.

In the book they are highlighted at the most likely stage with a nice comforting **Hazard!** icon.

It's human

At the top of the previous list you'll see 'giving up'. While people blame a whole host of other factors, this is actually the principal reason for business failure. Yet amazingly, few other books address it. It's easy to talk about 'VAT thresholds' but advising you how to keep your spirits up while dealing with a bolshy customer at 7pm on a Friday night after a rubbish week, well that's not so straightforward.

So, throughout this book I've included sections on your 'Mojo meter'. These are my estimates of how you are likely to be feeling at each stage of your start-up journey, charting the highs and lows. Under each of them, I've included handy tips and hints on how to keep your chin up.

I've also tried to make it fun and humorous. Running a business will not always be easy, but it will be one of the most rewarding experiences of your life.

I wish you all good speed!

PHASE 1

Preparation

In this phase, we do all the ground work necessary before you launch your business.

Step 1 Brace yourself

Step 2 Work on your brilliant business idea

Step 3 Road test your idea

Step 4 Build your support network

Step 5 Your business plan

Step 6 Reduce your start-up costs

Step 7 Raise finance

Step 8 Take care of the small print

STEP 1

Brace yourself

In this step we'll:

1 *Test* what you want to get from your business, and why this matters.

2 Get an *insight* of what it's really like running a business.

3 Do a quick *audit* of your skills and gaps.

We'll also look at the two essential ingredients of a successful entrepreneur.

What's it like running a business?

There are many great things about running your own business. You might make serious amounts of money. You gain control over your own destiny. It gives you the flexibility to choose how and when you work. It also offers the chance to do what you love.

But what about the negatives? Can you handle the stress? There are certainly a lot of responsibilities when you start up. You have customers, suppliers and maybe even staff depending on you. But when you've done it once, you find it gets much easier as you grow. It can also involve hard work. But this is balanced with the freedom to take off whenever you want. You don't have to stick to the old 9 to 5.

I also believe that in one sense, it's a lot less stressful than having a job. You are in control of your own destiny. Sure, it's your fault if things go wrong, but you also have everything in your power to fix them. I've never had a 'proper' job, but I figure that running my own business is a lot easier than having an idiot in charge of me, or being stuck in a hierarchy where I can't control what's happening to me – that's what I'd call stress!

Begin with the end in mind

Before you start, it's worth taking a few moments to think about your objective. If you just want a good life, then I'd perhaps not focus on growing large, but be smaller, specialised and very profitable. If you want to sell your business, then think about the buyer. Just because you've built a business, doesn't automatically mean other people will want to buy it. I've known people spend 30 years of their life building something no-one wants.

> if you want to sell your business, then think about the buyer

The most likely reasons someone will buy your business are:

- it gives them access to a high growth market
- you complement their product/service range (and it's too hard for them to add this themselves)
- they want your proprietary product or brand
- you're an annoyance to them, and they want you to go away.

So, if you want to sell for mega-bucks, you have to consider the following from the beginning:

- Think who your potential purchaser is likely to be (why not call and ask them?).

- Start building assets in your business. This doesn't necessarily mean equipment. It's unique things: a technology or process, a brand, a customer list, a unique set of relationships no-one can buy.

- Make yourself redundant. If the business is totally reliant on your doing a certain task or job, then no-one is going to want to buy it. Build systems that mean the business can function without you.

▶ brilliant example

A while back, small City PR firms were being bought-out for mega-bucks. It was because they wrote the chief executive's speeches for large companies. The big ad agencies who bought them figured they could use that trusted relationship to flog many more services to the customers.

Do you have what it takes?

There is no such thing as a *typical* entrepreneur. Show me a born hustler who worked his way up from an orphanage without a qualification to his name, and I'll show you a PhD student from a wealthy family who'd rather eat her own arm before making a sales call.

You don't have to be good at everything, but that's not to say your business can be unbalanced. You can be the world's greatest IT guru, but you are not getting anywhere if you never make a sales call, or run out of cash. For your business to grow, you need attention to all the areas. The secret is that you don't have to do it all yourself.

Everyone has strengths and weaknesses. Don't beat yourself up about it. In fact, you will often find your greatest weakness is often your greatest skill in reverse. But you must be aware of where your weak spots lie, and compensate for them. Otherwise they can make your business capsize.

It's also important to distinguish between skills and personality. While you can learn a new skill, it's far harder to change your personality.

brilliant example

You don't know much about book-keeping. That's fine, you can go on a quick course to swot up on this. If, however, you are not naturally a 'details person', you'll perhaps keep your books going for a few months before they spin out of control. The quicker you can delegate this task the better.

As you think through your abilities, be realistic about the skills you can pick up, and your basic psychological make-up which will indicate areas you'll have to compensate for.

Don't worry about being 'perfect'

There are so many jobs to do in a start-up it can seem daunting. The important thing is knowing which jobs to leave half done. It's easy for me because I'm naturally lazy, but as my father once said to me: 'The best is the enemy of the good.' You can spend so long making one thing perfect, like the type size in your business plan, that you miss out on so many other things that would make you successful.

> the important thing is knowing which jobs to leave half done

There is however one thing you need which is non-negotiable.

Passion

You don't have to be super-human to succeed. You certainly don't have to be well qualified. But there is one thing you need in abundance – passion. You may call it by its other names: drive, initiative, enthusiasm, motivation. But it's all about taking massive positive action.

This desire can come from many places. A burning need to escape poverty, to provide for your family, to impress the opposite sex, to prove a teacher wrong.

▶ brilliant example

One of the biggest financial battles of recent years was the attempt to take over Sainsbury's by the Three Delta fund. Led by millionaire former bricklayer Paul Taylor, the fund's name came from his class at school which his headteacher said would never amount to anything.

Wherever it comes from, this is the one part of entrepreneurship that can't be taught. And it is probably the most important ingredient of success.

There are a few things you can do however to sharpen your passion:

● Before you start, take time to ponder what success means *to you*. Don't be distracted by what other people term 'success'. It doesn't have to mean a gold-plated Ferrari. It could be 'retire by 45', or 'running a stable in Australia'. I met a talented entrepreneur whose ambition was to be on the first commercial space flight. She knew the date, and the price.

● Make your goals *crystal clear*. The more you can sharpen the focus on your destination, the more likely it is to come true. Some people help this process by pinning a picture of 'success' on their wall.

- Don't worry about how you will get there. Once you definitely commit to your big destination, your rational day-to-day brain will figure out the details. The whole point is that your dream is big and scary!

Swallow a 'brave pill'

There's no escaping it. To get more than everyone else, you have to take more of a risk.

Risk in business comes wearing many different hats:

- **Financial risk**. The risk of losing your home or savings. Though the most mentioned, this one is actually pretty easy to side step (see Step 7). It is often used as a smoke-screen for the other risks.

- **Being seen to fail**. Most people's fear of failure is one of being laughed at by family and friends. We'll get round that by building a support network in Step 4.

- **Fear of being different**. To get noticed as a small business, you will have to stand out from the crowd, and take more of a risk with your marketing and product. We cover that in Step 16.

- **Fear of rejection**. I'm afraid it's inevitable you will face. rejection. People will hang up on your sales calls, customers will leave for your competitors, staff will resign. It doesn't stop hurting, but I promise you it does get much, much easier.

But ultimately, profit is the reward for risk.

So, are you ready?

brilliant recap

Here are the exercises you've completed:

- You've conducted an audit of your skills, and have an idea of areas you might need support in.
- You've thought a bit harder about your destination.
- You've swallowed a 'brave pill'!

STEP 2

Work on your brilliant business idea

In this step, we cover your business idea.

1 If you don't have a business idea, we look at some places to find one.

2 We look at how to supercharge your idea.

   ● We check it genuinely meets customer needs.

   ● We also look at simple ways to protect it.

3 Finally, we pick a good name for the business.

How to come up with a good business idea

Look very hard for problems

The best business ideas don't come out of laboratories, they come in response to a customer's unsolved needs. Keep your ears open for problems. The larger they are, the bigger your potential business. It can help if you know a particular industry or customer group inside out, as this can get you closer to such problems.

brilliant example

Keith Mills was running a smallish advertising agency in London. He had British Airways and American Express for clients. American Express wanted a new reward for its members. BA then mentioned how it had spare capacity on its flights and were wondering what to do with it. He put two and two together and came up with 'Air Miles', and went on to build an international business. He recently sold out, netting a personal fortune of over £150 million.

often a fresh pair of eyes can see the obvious

But don't worry if you are not in an industry. Often a fresh pair of eyes can see the obvious solution that all the incumbents are too close to notice.

Listen out for phrases like: 'If only...', 'I wish', or 'We can't do that'. Get people to describe their dream product or service, or describe their biggest annoyance.

Look for change

Change is your friend. Many opportunities pop up when industries or populations go through periods of change. This can include:

- **New legislation**. For example, climate change will bring with it rafts of government legislation. This will throw up many opportunities for nimble start-ups.

- **Health/living trends**. When the economy does well, there is a move for 'premiumisation' – giving basic products a 'posh makeover'. Ice-cream got the Häagen Dazs makeover, coffee by Starbucks, chocolate by Green and Blacks, beefburgers are currently being tarted up. What else could do with a makeover? Two great websites for this are

www.trendwatching.com and **www.springwise.com** which publish trends and business ideas from around the world.

- **New technology**. This can open up new markets, but a word of warning. It's easy to get seduced by the excitement of new technology. But before plunging in head first, always ask: 'What fundamental problem is this technology solving?' Technology often has the habit of being a £2,000 answer to a £200 question.

Look overseas

Many brilliant ideas are simply imported. Perhaps you've found something on holiday or a work trip you think would be brilliant in the UK?

brilliant example

An American couple moved from Seattle to London and missed their coffee so much, they launched the Seattle Coffee Company, hiring space in Waterstone's bookshops. A few years later they sold out to Starbucks, and were one of the few people to make money out of the coffee boom (other than city centre landlords).

However, be aware of the often subtle cultural variations that exist.

brilliant example

After studying in the US, I set up the first student yearbook company in the UK. However, the US had large amounts of 'collegiate spirit' while most British students only wanted to remember their specific course, and were more interested in 'snog charts' than exam league tables!

Sometimes, it isn't enough just to 'love it'

There is no doubt that loving something makes your days go much faster. But a word of caution: *just because you love something doesn't mean there is a market for it.*

brilliant example

I sit on a funding panel for The Prince's Scottish Youth Business Trust. In one day we had two Polish restaurants looking for funding. Their rationale? 'We love Polish food!' That's fine, but their target market is Scottish customers. There are already three Polish restaurants in Edinburgh, and the local Tesco store has devoted half an aisle to Polish food.

There is a risk that making a living out of your hobby might just ruin your hobby.

Use your creativity to think of ways to make a valid business out of your passion. For some great examples of how to do this, I recommend reading *How I Made It* by Rachel Bridge. It's packed full of creative ways people have managed to turn their interests into successful businesses including antique lights, deep sea diving, and children's theatre.

Now supercharge your idea

You have your business idea: that's where most start-ups stop. But we're not most start-ups! We don't want to end up just another 'me-too' business. We want to make our business unique, the best in the market, and miles ahead of the competition.

So we need to supercharge our proposition. The following are some simple but extremely effective ways to do this.

Go niche

People tell you to 'think big' when you start up. It's great to be ambitious, but it can be more valuable to 'think small'. You don't want to be the Ford of business: big, lumbering and loss-making. Your model should be Porsche: small, specialised and the most profitable car company in the world. So, think of ways to specialise your business into tightly defined niches.

There are many benefits to being niche:

- you can charge more for your specialist services
- you have a great competitive advantage over 'generalists'
- word of your specialism will spread
- you can invest in specialist equipment and knowledge, rather than being confined to a life of mediocrity
- you can work anywhere, and it's easier to expand geographically.

It's also relatively easy and cheap to specialise. Often a 'specialist' service just requires a more detailed understanding of your specific market niche, and small tailoring of the service to fit.

brilliant example

You have a window cleaning business. How about a specialist service for tall buildings, or retail shop windows which includes a paint retouching and graffiti removal service?

So if it's so easy, why don't more start-ups do it? Usually the following worries put them off pursuing a niche strategy.

brilliant questions and answers

Q Will I have to turn-away customers who don't fit my tightly defined niche?

A If they are existing customers, they won't care what you call yourself. You can set up a sub-brand for your specialist niche (e.g. banks have units for charities, aircraft leasing, agriculture).

Q Is it a risk to have all my 'eggs in one basket'?

A There is a risk that sectors take a down-turn, but you should be able to weather the storm and emerge stronger. And in most economic down-turns, there are few sectors that remain completely unscathed.

Q Will my clients be worried about a conflict of interest?

A The actual worry clients may have is one of confidentiality, and it's easier to reassure them on this. Most clients will value the specialism more. As a client once said: 'Two clients is a conflict. Three is a specialism.' Bear in mind, you can't expect to win every customer you go for. Far better you have a few very high paying specialist customers.

Gender niches

One niche you might want to consider is sex. While differences between genders become blurred, that doesn't mean there isn't money to be had in exploiting them.

brilliant global examples

It's not just the bottle shape of Poland's Karmi beer that's different. It comes in sweeter flavours than mainstream beers, such as pineapple and caramel. It also has a lower calorie count, the same as natural yoghurt. It's all part of a successful venture to tap into a female beer market.

And it works both ways. Noticing her friends were fed up that their husbands didn't have the time or skills to fix things around the house, a canny Australian entrepreneur set up 'Hire a Hubby'. They're now expanding their fix-it business around the world.

Make your product/service unique

We live in a land of bland. Large companies spend a fortune on churning out undistinguishable me-too products because they are too large, scared or lazy to take a risk. Your willingness to take a risk is your one great advantage.

The more unique your offering, the easier it is to sell. This uniqueness can come from a range of places. It can be in your product design, such as the Dyson vacuum or iPod, or it can be in the channel you use to deliver it.

 **example**

Ted Smart realised there was a huge market for people who liked books, but never visited a bookshop. So he set up a business taking the books direct to them – in their offices and factories around the UK. Today, The Book People has a turnover in excess of £100 million and sells 20 million books a year.

Alternatively, it could be an extra element of your service no-one offers.

 **example**

William Seyssel had been a barber for 25 years. Then he hit on a great way to differentiate his business. He cuts people's hair with a flick-knife. Rockabillies and others rush to his business and he's had good press coverage.

You can also make yourself unique through the experience you give your customers.

brilliant global example

US ice-cream store Cold Stone Creamery gets its customers really involved in making their ice-creams. They mix the flavours together on a large cold stone. They also hire actors to make the experience lively and unforgettable.

brilliant tip

Don't assume the competition will stand still

I dropped out of an Economics degree, partly in frustration with one phrase I kept hearing: *ceteris paribus* (which means other things being equal). To see an effect, most economic theories assume all other things will stay the same. Well, that's fine in a textbook. But in real life, that's the last thing that will happen.

Many small businesses fall into the same trap. They assume they can make a small change, such as being 10 per cent cheaper or offering free delivery and assume this is a 'killer advantage'. They forget that if you are successful, the competition will immediately copy you, and they'll probably have deeper pockets.

So make sure your advantage is genuinely unique, and that it is hard for your competitors to copy. And if they do, it won't matter, because you will be onto your next innovation.

Turn your 'features' into 'benefits'

It's very easy to get excited by all the excellent features your product/service has but now you have to stand on your head.

features count for nothing – start with the benefits

Features count for nothing – you have to start with what the 'benefits' are for your customers.

A great example of this not happening is in the computer industry. For years manufacturers obsessed about cramming more gigs, rams and hertz into their products. Now I don't know about you, but so long as my computer goes, I don't really care if it's powered by hamsters. But show me the Apple MacBook that fits in an envelope and I start to drool.

I'll repeat this: don't start with your product, and try and load it with things. Start with your customer, and think what they want.

And don't think the obvious. Many a stereo system has been bought on its potential to get its owner laid.

The following three-stage exercise should help.

Stage one

In the first column, make a list of the main five features of your offering. In the right column translate this feature into a benefit for your customers:

Feature	Benefit to the customer
Example: I use a stronger wood to make my office furniture.	Example: My furniture is built to last you a lifetime.
1.	
2.	
3.	
4.	
5.	

Stage two

Forget your existing product and think – what *might* your customers really want? These are potentially features no-one has ever thought of before. For example, 'I'm a high-flying corporate executive. I want my desk to signify my prowess, and make visitors cower at my magnificence.' Now think what additional features you could build in to satisfy these wants:

Potential untapped need	Potential new feature
Example: To show off to other colleagues.	Example: My desks are made from rare Amazonian Nogga-Nogga wood, traditionally only used for tribal chiefs.
1.	
2.	
3.	
4.	
5.	

Stage three

Rerank the features of your offering based on which are the most important needs of your target audience. Chances are you might have to design some new features into your offering. That's great. It shows you are truly innovating and ahead of the competition.

Stop for a moment and think: what business are you actually in?
If you become a 'benefit ninja', you can take this approach to a higher level. Very few businesses ever do this, but those that do find it revolutionises their model. Forget the sector you are in. Start only with what your customer is actually buying from you.

▶ brilliant example

Parker realised it was not a pen company – it was a gift company. Most people buy pens not because they want something to write with, but because they want to buy a gift for someone.

This revolution in thinking can change several factors:

- How you price your product. 'I'm happy to spend £35 on Uncle Walter.' Average pen price: £35.
- Who your competition is. 'Perhaps Uncle Walter would like a new golf club instead of a pen...'
- Where to market your product. 'Good job I read this in-flight magazine, I would never have thought of a pen otherwise.'

Make your brand and marketing brilliant

You have a niche offering, and it genuinely stands out from your competition. Now you have to make your marketing explosive. I'm not just talking about a clever advert you produce a year down the line. (We cover 'promotion' in Step 16.) I'm talking about embracing explosive thinking at the very core of your business.

you have to make your marketing explosive

You probably think your offering is pretty special anyway. You're bound to – it's your baby. But think back to the last time you recoiled from a friend's pram: babies are not always as beautiful as their parents might believe.

Seriously, you mustn't underestimate how much 'noise' there is competing for your customers' attention. It is estimated that the average person is exposed to 3,000 marketing messages a day. You have to cut through all of this to get noticed. You can't do this just by 'shouting louder' than everyone else – after all, the competition for your driving school is not the driving school up the road, it's the billboard your prospect is looking at instead. Again, it's time for some smarter thinking, and taking more of a risk in the packaging and promotion of your offering.

Big companies have big budgets, but there is no guarantee of a big idea. In fact, quite the opposite. The larger a company is, the less of a risk it tends to take.

---

brilliant example

Belinda Jarron's business is supplying plants and flowers to offices. But her largest competitor is Rentokil – a $2 billion turnover giant. One of Belinda's weapons is her brilliant marketing. She has called her business 'Fleurtations' and has bright pink vans, and staff in matching uniforms. She has had no problem competing successfully against Rentokil.

Of course, it is not that easy to become a risk taker overnight. But there are some exercises that help.

Three steps to becoming more adventurous

1 *Ignore your existing customers.* You have to silence the lurking worry. 'What will my closest customers think of this?' Nervous of their possible reaction, you play it safe.

   Stop thinking of what they 'might' say. They're working with you already. Instead, start with the people who don't know you. Think how adventurous you are going to have to be to hook their attention.

2 *Don't apologise for who you are.* Don't think, 'I'm selling to bigger companies so I've got to pretend to be big.' Nonsense. You've got a far bigger problem of getting noticed in the first place. There are many ways to reassure them once you have (see Step 9).

3 *Get some distance from your marketing.* Literally. Pin your proposition on a wall along with your competitors. Ask a stranger to pick the one they notice first.

brilliant examples

1 A litmus test used by advertising agencies is to put a new advert down the end of a dimly-lit corridor. If the unique selling point or hook is visible from there then they are on to a winner. If you can't see it, then you need to 'turn up the volume'.

2 Advertising genius David Ogilvy talked about a 'burr of singularity' – a single point that sticks in a customer's mind. He produced a series of adverts for men's shirts in which the model wore an eye-patch. It intrigued people and sales shot up.

If the target audience is right for it then you can use stunts if you want to.

brilliant example

At the height of the dotcom bomb, and keen to cash in, I launched a magazine on e-commerce. There are over 1,000 business magazines in the UK, and 'those in the know' reckon you need a marketing budget of £700,000 to launch a new one. We had £700.

So I decided to launch it by spending a week living in a shop window surviving off the internet. I started in my pyjamas, with a credit card and computer in a shop window in Sauchiehall Street in Glasgow.

▶

I had a number of challenges to complete. I had to order food (£40 from Iceland – lot of food, no freezer). I organised a dinner party. I got a barber to come in, a six-foot wooden giraffe, pipe band and vintage Bentley. The only challenge I failed was from my sister – to get a glass of ice.

I also drew quite a crowd. I had two drunks who adopted me and would post sandwiches through the letter box. I got my own stalker who would smile enigmatically, and a group of night clubbers – one of whom shouted something about a 'job' she would give me if I let her in. I couldn't quite work it out.

Of course, this wasn't an exercise in e-commerce, it was an exercise in hype. I was in all the main papers (I got my three-month old daughter in *The Sun*), on TV, had a radio station based in the window with me, and about 1,000 e-mails a day. We also got more subscribers than any other Scottish magazine launch.

Now come up with a good name for your business

In truth, you can call your business almost anything and it won't matter much. After all, Tesco was named after their first supplier's name and it's hardly held them back. However, we are smart businesses, so we want all the advantages we can get.

To pick a good name, follow similar approaches.

Start with the customer need and not the product feature

This is a great chance to convey what is unique about your offer, as opposed to who you are or where you're based. Compare two advertising agencies:

- 'Story' – an agency that sells its client's products by telling really engaging stories about them (tagline 'the best selling agency', with a website that reads like a children's adventure).
- 'Faulds' – an agency started by Jim Faulds.

But a word of caution. Think of the need that your customer has. A boring name might be fine if the main thing the customer wants is reassurance. But if you are selling creativity, that won't do. Hence advertising agencies are known by perplexing anagrams of names and initials like 'Beagle Bimble and Numbnuts', rather than 'Sales Edge' because they want to convey the creative flair of a few mavericks, and not a dull factory.

> think of the need that your customer has

Make it memorable

Clearly, you're not the first person to think about naming a business after a benefit. But the trick is to make it stick in the mind:

● Bad: 'Mavis King Ironing Services'
● Better: 'Speedy Iron'
● Best: 'The Iron Lady'

It doesn't have to be funny, but it helps to have something that lodges in people's brains. They'll remember you, and they'll talk about you. This should save you a fortune in advertising.

brilliant example

One of my earlier businesses was an event organising company I called 'Let Me Hold Your Balls For You'. I got loads of calls. Some of them were even about work.

Protect yourself

Have you protected your idea?

You've put a lot of effort into supercharging your idea. So it's worth protecting it. There are a number of ways to do this, some legal and expensive, some practical and cheap.

Register your design

You have automatic rights on the design of your product: for example, this can be its distinctive shape. It has to demonstrate 'free thought' – so you haven't just copied an idea from elsewhere.

You should consider registering your design with the UK Intellectual Property Office (**www.ipo.gov.uk**; tel: 0300 300 2000). This isn't a requirement, but it makes it easier to defend, otherwise you have to rely on the common law of 'passing off' to protect your idea. It's not an expensive process. Also, on any marketing material, include the fact you have registered your design to deter others.

Post yourself anything copyrighted

You also have automatic copyright for anything artistic you have created. This includes obvious things like music and film, but can also include information booklets and computer programs. The simplest way to prove prior ownership is to put your material into a well-sealed envelope, post it to yourself by Special Delivery (which gives you proof of delivery) and then don't open the envelope, but keep it somewhere safe.

To deter others, put the © symbol on your work, along with your name and the date.

Trade marks

This is a mark that distinguishes your product from your competitors'. This can be your logo, wording, signs or sounds. It is slightly more difficult to register:

- First you must do a comprehensive search to see that no-one else has your trade mark.

- You then apply to the Intellectual Property Office as above. Make sure you get it right first time, as you cannot alter it once registered. Also, specify all the uses you want to apply this trade mark to. If successful, you will get 10 years' protection initially, after which you can reregister.

- Then put your ™ mark on your most obvious places. (Please don't do the annoying thing some brand holders think of and use it at every opportunity.) Even a Brilliant Start-up™ can become a Brilliant Pain-in-the-™ if overused.

Domain names

Having a trade mark does not automatically confer on you the right to a domain name, providing the holder is not passing themselves off to infringe your mark. Similarly, a domain name does not confer a trade mark.

> a domain name does not confer a trade mark

brilliant example

The most subscribed magazine in the world is *The Economist*. But take a look at **www.theeconomist.com**.

Once you have your unique name, try to buy up all the domains associated with it, even if you have to be creative with your wording.

Only consider a patent if it's genuinely unique

This gives you 20 years' protection of your idea. However, patents are by no means easy or cheap to come by and there are significant hurdles to be overcome.

You will need to meet one of three criteria:

1 A new technology.
2 A new piece of equipment.
3 A new business process.

Business process patents are an area of considerable debate and legislation. For example, Amazon claims a patent for its 'one-click' ordering process.

You cannot patent an idea, discovery or an artistic work. Your proposition must be capable of being made. It also has to be a genuinely 'inventive step' – something which is not obvious to someone in your field.

It typically takes two to three years to apply for a patent, there are significant costs in applying, it will only apply to a limited geography, and you have to be prepared to go to court to defend it.

Be first and fast

brilliant example

The chief executive of one of the UK's leading companies was asked what his competitive advantage was. His answer was 'two months'. It's how long the company thinks it will take the competition to catch up with it, and the speed at which it will have to react.

For most businesses you'll find your best protection is being first on the market, taking a dominant position and building unassailable relationships with your customers.

Keep quiet

The other great way of protecting your idea/clients is not to let your competitors know about them. We'll come on to ways of ensuring this in Step 4.

Give it away

There is an alternative to protecting your intellectual property – give it away.

---

brilliant global examples

While studying in Belgium, Dries Buytaert set up a website for a group of his friends. As he couldn't afford the software to build it, he wrote his own. Soon others began to ask him for copies of it as they were building their own, so Dries decided to give away his program.

Today Drupal has been downloaded over 2 million times and drives thousands of websites, including the White House's. Dries has set up a company to support this user community, and landed millions of dollars in funding to do it.

And it's an approach that can work beyond software. For example, Canadian mining company Goldcorp published its survey maps online and offered to share the rewards with anyone who could analyse the maps to find new gold deposits.

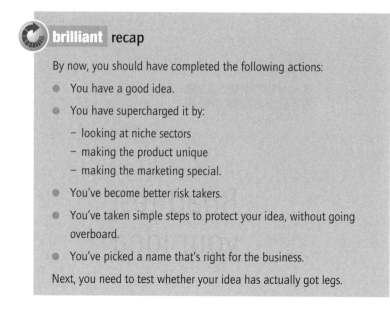

brilliant recap

By now, you should have completed the following actions:

● You have a good idea.

● You have supercharged it by:

  – looking at niche sectors
  – making the product unique
  – making the marketing special.

● You've become better risk takers.

● You've taken simple steps to protect your idea, without going overboard.

● You've picked a name that's right for the business.

Next, you need to test whether your idea has actually got legs.

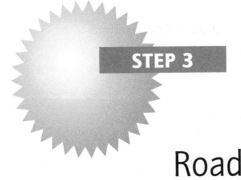

STEP 3

Road test your idea

In this step, your idea steps out of the shadows and meets the real world.

1 We'll look at four ways to test your idea.
2 You'll inevitably hit some brick walls, so we look at some essential ways to keep your mojo up.
3 Finally, we have a quick look at alternatives to starting from scratch.

Does your idea have legs?

It's been fun so far, hasn't it? You are probably buzzing with the potential of your business. People are bound to love it. You are going to be massive!

I don't want to spoil the party, but you are just coming to the end of the honeymoon period. We now have to check your idea actually has legs. We have to test some of the fairly massive assumptions we've made so far. This is more important if you're entering an industry you know little about. Things which look easy on the outside are actually a lot harder to achieve when you get closer to the problem.

there is no 'market in the gap'

Another common risk is that you've spotted a 'gap in the market', but there is no 'market in the gap'. There's often a very good reason no-one has stepped in to fill the void. Don't let this put you off. It's often people from outside an industry who come up with the new ideas. But there's certainly time for a reality check.

brilliant example

A dotcom company cornered the market for delivering goods in 60 minutes. The problem was the market in the gap. They were often delivering things like aspirins and condoms worth £2, when delivery alone cost £2.50.

How to research your target market

There are four options for market research. The first two most people use and are pretty useless. The final two we are going to use.

Useless method 1: desk research

This is the approach you would have been taught in business school. You start with Google and put in a search for your business: 'gooseberry juice'. You find there aren't many places selling it. Great – no competition! So you widen your search, and you come across an industry report: 'UK Fruit Juice Market'. Things start to get exciting. It says, 'the UK fruit juice market is £900 million'. Wow! And what's more 'there is increasing demand for unusual juices'. Just like you knew there was! You don't want to be overly optimistic, but you figure 0.1 per cent of the market is yours for the taking. That's nearly £1 million! Get stuck in!

You will see the obvious flaw in this approach. This doesn't prove a single person is interested in buying your juice. It seems obvious, but you'd be amazed how many otherwise intelligent people fall into this trap. Remember, this isn't research to convince a bank manager, it's too important for that. You are about to bet the next few years of your life on this. So let's move on to the next mistake I've made.

Almost useless method 2: field research

At least you've got off your comfy chair. You are out in the street. You are maybe counting the number of people walking past your potential site. You might even pluck up the courage to speak to a couple of them about your new venture.

There are flaws in this. Take the example of a restaurant. People going past a site is no guarantee they will stop and eat. This explains 'white elephant' sites that change hands every few years. They're usually on busy junctions that no-one can get to, or on commuter routes when people are hurrying home. And people tell you what they think you want to hear. Why would they tell you the truth and risk hurting your feelings?

---

brilliant example

Before producing my first yearbook, I went round asking people if they'd buy one, how much they'd pay and what they'd want in it. I then designed a book around this feedback.

However, I found that telling a friend you'd spend £10 on their lovely idea is very different from actually handing over £10 that could more usefully be spent on beer.

I also found that the actual customers were their parents, and they weren't so impressed with photos of darling Johnny with his pants on his head.

So that takes us to the third method.

Surprisingly good method 3: ask the competition

It's a common mistake to aim for an area where there is no competition. Competition is your friend. It shows that there is demand for your product that you don't have to create from scratch. With your supercharged idea, you are going to beat the competition anyway.

competition is your friend

There are lots of secret squirrel ways you can find things out about the competition, but the most effective is just to ask them directly. You'll be amazed at how much they'll tell you. Business owners love to talk about themselves. They'll probably not see you as a threat. Perhaps they'll figure on you developing the market so they can take your customers later. And the worst they can say is 'no' – you've lost nothing for asking. But it might help if your competitor is in a different geographic location.

You could go and work for a competitor. That's fine if it's a large business, or in a very different location, but don't do it in an underhand way to a small business near you. Just you wait until someone does it to you.

Alternatively, ask the competition's customers directly. What do they think of the industry? What would they look for in a supplier that no-one is giving them?

Which brings us to the final method.

Outstanding method 4: make a prototype and sell it

The only real way to check demand for your offering is to sell it. This may seem the wrong way round – selling your product before you've set up – but it's a brilliantly effective way to gauge its potential.

brilliant example

A group of friends bought some fruit, and set up a stall at a music festival in London. They made smoothies, and in front of their booth put two waste bins and a sign saying 'Do you think we should give up our jobs to make these smoothies?' At the end, the 'yes' bin was full of empty cartons. They went on to set up Innocent Drinks, a £100 million plus company.

You might think this is 'amateurism', that you should commit properly. But it's an essential way to buy yourself time and space to get things wrong, and avoid the Law of Unintended Consequences.

The Law of Unintended Consequences . . .

Or how one action often causes a completely unforeseen opposite reaction.

Look at mobile phones. The networks ploughed billions into whizzy 3G technology, which hasn't come close to repaying the investment. But customers have fallen in love with clunky text messaging.

The danger you face as a start-up is that you spend too long locked in your laboratory/bedroom perfecting your master plan, without checking what customers actually want to do with it.

Great, but how do you do it? It looks tricky, but you just need a bit of creative thinking. Remember, this isn't necessarily a fully functioning product/service. It can simply be an outline that gives you a good idea of what the customer thinks.

brilliant global example

Benson & Hedges were developing its cigarette boxes. It hit on the idea of solid gold boxes, but its customers said they hated them. But one maverick pressed ahead, and made some mock-ups. When put in front of customers he noted that whatever they might say, they couldn't resist picking up and handling the boxes. A global brand was born.

A service business is perhaps easiest to 'prototype'. You describe your offering to customers and look for their reaction. If you have a product, you make a dummy of it. Suppliers might be able to do a mock-up for you. You can even prototype a retail business. Instead of opening your new shop, it might be possible to sub-let a small amount of space in someone else's. Many multi-million pound retailers have started this way (see Step 6).

However you do it, the idea is to make your mistakes on the cheap before you invest heavily in the real thing.

Get your customers to complain

You are sitting in a restaurant, having a grim meal, vowing never to return. The waiter comes over with a 'Is everything OK with your meal?' You smile and nod weakly. Don't let this happen to your business. You have to know exactly what your customers think about your offering. The problem is, people are often too polite to give you bad news to your face.

There are ways round this:

- Start by asking them what they like. Then they'll be happier to give you the bad news.

- Get someone like a friend to do it for you. They might tell them things they wouldn't to your face.

You never know, you might even get a nice surprise.

brilliant example

We quoted for a job with a large credit card company. I grilled the contact about our proposal. He was complimentary up to a point, and then added, 'You also appear to have sent us your costs, not your price.' That set us thinking.

Mojo meter: are you hitting a brick wall?

At the start of this chapter you were probably feeling pretty gung-ho about your new business. However, if you've done your research properly, you've probably taken a bit of a battering by now. You've found your competitors are not quite the dullards you once thought they were. Your ideas are not quite so nice and shiny now. This is one of the crunch times for your business. It's when far too many people pack it in. It's vital that you don't feel defeated by this.

Hurdles are good: they are opportunities in disguise. They are what will keep others out of your business. If you haven't found two or three 'insurmountable brick walls' then you are probably not looking hard enough. Don't despair, there is always a way round them. After all, we don't remember Richard Branson as Britain's best student newspaper publisher.

If things look hopeless, perhaps you need to rethink your approach. This is called 'getting from A to C, without going through B'.

NASA needed to find a way for astronauts to write in space. The problem was that the ink flow of pens depended on gravity. So they invested millions of dollars in a special zero-gravity ink propulsion system.

The Russians looked at the same problem. They used a pencil.

A quick word on alternatives

This is a start-up book, so I've focused on starting from scratch but, there are some other options.

Buying a business

This can obviously save you a lot of the leg work. It's best if someone is retiring, and they can pass on perhaps premises, equipment and a solid customer base. I'd sound a couple of words of caution however:

- *Caveat emptor*: literally 'buyer beware'. It's up to you to do your homework into the business. There is no requirement for the seller to tell you of any hidden minefields.

- Question their motivations for selling. If it's such a great business, why are they not sticking with it? Perhaps one of their major customers is about to leave? Perhaps their equipment is clapped out?

And don't be put off starting from scratch – it's not as hard as you think. It's also an invaluable learning opportunity.

Spinning out

You might be working for a large bloated company. Perhaps they have a division which makes a great small business, but doesn't appear on their radar screens. This can be a fantastic opportunity for starting-up. Try approaching the owners or senior managers and offer to 'spin-out' the business. You can pay them a lump

offer to 'spin-out' the business

sum, a licence fee or share of future revenues. I've heard some amazing stories of people being *paid* to take distracting business units off the hands of larger companies.

But if they're not willing to play ball? Well, you are quite entitled to leave and set up on your own.

Buying a franchise

brilliant definition

Franchising

Franchising is basically using somebody else's system to run a business.

People used to be sniffy about franchising, saying they're not 'proper' businesses. Fortunately those days are long gone. There are over 30,000 franchised outlets in the UK and over 93 per cent claim to be profitable.

The benefits of a franchise are that you are getting a tried and tested concept, and a proven brand, so you can hit the ground running. You also get support, training and the chance to share in best practice. Of course, there's a cost to this hand-holding. Financially, you will usually have to pay an initial franchise fee, and then a management services fee or royalty, an advertising levy and/or a mark-up on everything you sell.

There are also other non-financial 'costs'. Running a franchise is more restrictive – the franchisor will have systems you will have to adhere to, performance levels you will have to meet, and they will be able to inspect you.

If your main interest in running a business is to earn a good regular income then franchising is something you should look at seriously. If, on the other hand, you want a higher degree of freedom and flexibility then perhaps it's not for you.

See the British Franchise Association website **www.thebfa.org** for a guide to all things franchising.

brilliant recap

Assumptions are too risky, so you've researched your idea properly. Having ignored the two useless forms of research, you have instead:

● Asked the competition for their insight.

● Made a prototype and tried to sell it.

STEP 4

Build your support network

Things are going well:

- you've got a brilliant idea
- you've supercharged it
- you've road tested it.

In fact, your 'research' might have gone so well that you've accidentally started in business already! But there's a valuable step people often overlook: you need to build a support network.

In this step:

1 We look at how to get a coach.
2 We use expert professionals and obtain a mentor.
3 We consider some inspirational people.

Mojo meter: surround yourself with cheerleaders

brilliant definition

A success

Someone who gets up one more time than they fall over.

Too many small businesses fail simply because the founders stop getting up. There can be valid business reasons for this, but often it's simply that they've had enough.

Isolation is one of your greatest dangers in a start-up. You've been having a hard day in your business – a machine has broken and you've got a tight deadline. You're feeling a bit under the weather. Then another customer phones up to complain. You begin to wonder if this entrepreneurship stuff is all it's cracked up to be.

That's why you need a support network for your business – a 'dream team' if you like. Don't worry, this isn't difficult or expensive. Ideally it should include:

- a 'coach' to listen to your problems, help you think things through and be a general cheerleader for you
- experts to advise on specialist topics where they have far more experience than you
- inspiration to keep you going.

What's more, you needn't pay a penny for it!

Your 'coach'

It's often possible to think things through in your own mind only so far. Then you need someone to talk things through with. By having to explain things to someone else, you clarify matters for yourself. Note that I'm not saying 'give you advice'. That's often the last thing you need. Nine times out of 10, you know the answer, you just need to 'discover' it. The other risk with advice is you end up relying too much on it and not trusting your own powerful intuition. It's also great just to have someone to share your misery with. Not for nothing is psychiatry called the 'talking cure'.

> nine times out of 10, you know the answer

So, who is the wondrous person who'll put up with all your moaning?

Paid for listening

You could pay for a 'sounding board'. There are lots of professional 'life coaches' who do just this. But there are cheaper alternatives.

Other start-ups

This can be one of the best sources. There are hundreds of small business groups around the country. Do a search on Google – some of them are 'introduction' networks whose main aim is to get people selling to each other, but that might suit you anyway. See the *Useful contacts* for a link.

Bear in mind, you don't have to meet face to face. I know a group who phone each other every Friday morning for a chat, and will occasionally pop to the pub to share horror stories.

Don't tell your friends

OK, I'm being deliberately provocative, but only to make a serious point. Your support network might not be your closest friends. They might try to talk you out of your ventures with good (and sometimes bad) intentions. You also run the risk of boring them to tears. They're used to seeing you as 'Davey down the pub', they might not be ready for 'Davey the millionaire internet pioneer'. The risk is also that you sugar coat things for friends, when you need the unvarnished truth.

Think twice before setting up in business with a friend.

To get over this 'start-up loneliness', many people decide to start up in partnership with a colleague, friend or loved one. It's great in the short term to have a chum to share your worries with. But in the long run you might have seriously different ideas about the direction of the business. I've seen otherwise very successful businesses torn apart by warring partners.

Also, it's worth considering that unless your business is in Scotland, where the law is different, each individual is liable for the total debts of the business (see Step 8).

I was delighted when someone told me that the German for partnership is *Partnerschaft*.

So, before taking the plunge into partnership, go back to your personal audit in Step 1. If you are genuinely weak in one area, such as sales, then it can make sense to partner with someone who is strong in this area. But bear in mind this is a (business) life-long commitment. On the other hand, if your desire for a partner is more to have someone to share the stresses and strains, then get a good support network instead: or a dog.

Your team of experts

There are two types of these: 'professionals' and 'experienced entrepreneurs'.

Using professionals

As you will find, there are a lot of people making money in the advice game.

At best, they can be a very cost-effective way of avoiding a lot of future pain. At worst, they are an expensive way of telling you what you already knew. The problem is not with the wrong types of advisers, but with the wrong way of using them.

> there are a lot of people making money in the advice game

How to use lawyers and other professionals

Most professionals charge you for their time. This can mean you are being charged from the second they pick up the phone, however small the query. And these fees are not cheap.

brilliant example

A friend was using a planning lawyer, who charged £800 an hour, for a complex enquiry. Halfway through a meeting the lawyer got up to go to the loo. My friend and his colleagues looked at each other, then followed him into the toilet and continued the conversation over the cubicle wall.

I'm not knocking professionals, their advice is often worth many more times than what it costs, but use them intelligently.

brilliant tips

1 Take advice before you need it. It's worth seeing an accountant and a lawyer before starting in business. Our lawyers gave us a fantastic 'legal MOT'. In 90 minutes they did an audit of all the systems we had in place and things that needed tightening.

2 Try free sources first. There are lots of excellent sources of information on the web. This does not constitute tailored advice – think of it more of a way of doing your homework.

3 Then use cheaper sources. For example, the Federation of Small Businesses have an excellent legal advice line, which is covered in your annual membership and is worth the cost of membership alone. Other organisations will offer similar services. Banks often offer paid-for advice services on areas such as employment law and tax.

▶

4   Prepare. Write down the specific question you want answered. Gather all the documentary evidence. Tell them the outcome you want to achieve. (Quite often the best legal solution is not a legal solution.) If you are having a legal dispute, reaching a 'compromise agreement' where you both admit a degree of fault can be far better.

5   Swallow your pride and remember: 'If you go out seeking revenge, start by digging two graves.'

Get an experienced entrepreneur as a mentor

brilliant definition

Mentor

A mentor is someone who's done it before, and is willing to show you how.

If I had to reduce this book to two key steps, the first one would be sales, and this would be the second one.

A good mentor can save you months of work, show you the most obvious pitfalls to avoid and give you contacts. They might even invest in your business. So, you can see why you want one.

brilliant example

When I started up, The Prince's Trust found me a mentor via an organisation of retired professionals. My mentor had run a number of businesses before. One of his first bits of advice was 'double your price'. I did. It massively increased my profits, and amazingly, my sales went up.

You don't get that kind of advice in books (well, except for this one!).

You can have more than one

Don't get hung up on finding the perfect one person. You can have several people whose advice you take on marketing, manufacturing, strategy and so on.

Think laterally

Think broadly about the type of advice you need and can't get elsewhere. Ideally you want someone with specific experience in your sector, but don't be too blinkered. Say you want to open a clothes shop, you could do worse than speak to someone with a gift shop on the same road. They can give you guidance about shop fitting, local trades people, stock levels, design, regulations, lease negotiation and so on.

Don't expect them to hold your hand

We've already covered the people to use for a general moan and pep talk. This is *not* what your mentor is for. They are often far too busy, and it's a poor use of their time. You want your mentor for their insight.

you want your mentor for their insight

⏵ brilliant example

I have a mentor in Ray Perman, a brilliant publisher. He'd be alarmed to hear me call him that. All he thinks we do is meet for coffee once in a blue moon. In an hour, Ray can give me a year's worth of valuable advice.

Don't get heavy on your first date

The arrangement does not have to be a formal commitment. The mentor doesn't even have to know they are mentoring you. In fact, you don't have to speak to them more than once.

Don't ask mentors for money (unless they offer). Conversely, I wouldn't expect to pay them. Buy them lunch, or send them a small token of acknowledgement for their time.

Be prepared

If your mentor is successful, chances are you'll only have a limited amount of their time. So, make it pay. Think through the exact questions you want answers to, and ignore any waffly ones you can get answers from elsewhere. Don't just say, 'Have you got any ideas on how I can start up?'

▶ brilliant global example

A software developer in the US got the chance to meet the leading figure in his field for lunch. He spent two weeks formulating his questions, and asking others for what to ask his hero. During the lunch, he rattled through all his queries. The other guy was exhausted at the end, but extremely impressed. On the spot, he offered him the chance to come and shadow him in his company.

Where to find one

Once you have a list of the type of advice you need, start asking around. Look for people who've recently sold their businesses or retired. They'll love talking about their experiences, have a valuable sense of perspective, and should have more time. Ask your family, bank manager, suppliers, business support organisations (see *Useful contacts*). Ask your competitors (the worst they can say is no).

Set your sights high. Don't worry if you don't personally know the person, bear in mind the 'Six Degrees of Separation' – a theory that everyone in the world can be linked in six steps. Someone will know someone who knows someone.

Why supermodels have ugly boyfriends

While everyone else is too intimidated by their beauty, the cocky ones figure they have nothing to lose by asking them out. So don't worry they'll say no. If you've done your homework, and know your stuff, they're more likely to be impressed. And what's more – I bet people rarely ask them.

Using your public sector support agencies

Entrepreneurs give government support agencies a lot of stick. The main complaint is that they've no experience of running a business. I think that's not surprising, but you just have to approach them the right way.

brilliant dos and don'ts

Do

✔ Get them to guide you through any legal formalities.

✔ Ask about regional initiatives and good network opportunities.

✔ Listen to any advice they have on local business issues (suppliers, contacts, etc.).

✔ Plunder their other free resources, such as market research reports that would cost you a lot of money otherwise.

Don't

✘ Take as gospel their general advice on your business. You'll soon find everyone is an expert, but unless they've got detailed experience in your industry, I'd take their advice with a pinch of salt.

Keeping things 'hush-hush'

Hazard

You must stop people from nicking your brilliant idea.

In the course of your research you'll probably need to speak to potential customers, mentors, people in your market and suppliers. You'll be wanting to find good, commercially-minded people. The very people who might like the look of your idea so much, they do it themselves.

you can't be overly paranoid

This is no reason not to speak to them. You can't be overly paranoid. After all, your genius will be in the way you execute your plans. But there's no harm in being careful.

A simple way is to ask people to sign a non-disclosure agreement. Under the UK law of confidentiality, if you disclose information in confidence to people then they are bound not to reveal this if it is not already in the public domain. This can apply to anyone, including journalists and employees.

You can buy off-the-shelf templates for such agreements for as little as £7.35: See **www.compactlaw.co.uk/confidentiality-agreement.html**.

Get inspired!

The third area you can never get too much of is inspiration. There is nothing like hearing, watching or reading an inspiring story to spur you on with your efforts. It can also put your own worries in perspective.

example

I thought I'd done some adventurous things in my life. Then I met Miles Hilton-Barber. He's a polar explorer. He's flown from London to Sydney in a microlight. He's travelled around the world with a paraplegic (including scuba diving with him in the Red Sea). And he's walked unaided across the Sahara. Oh yes, and he's completely blind.

It's infectious spending time around such positive people. Go and hear them speak. Read interviews with them, buy their books (many successful entrepreneurs say their bookshelves are full of autobiographies of heroic people). Put up pictures around you, so next time you are feeling depressed because the printer cocked up your order, you can give thanks for the fact that you are not stuck in the Arctic Sea in a force-12 gale with a broken rudder.

recap

Your team should be ready now:

- You've sourced 'coaches' you can speak to for advice.
- You've thought wisely about how to use professionals.
- You have tracked down a mentor.
- You have a source of great inspirational stories.

STEP 5

Your business plan

In this step:

1 We look at the simplest of business plans.

2 We check your figures are realistic.

The only business plan you'll ever need

You've got a team of experts, entrepreneurs and support-ers to help you, now it's time to plan. I'm not a great fan of business plans. There are hundreds of books, websites and soft-ware packages you can buy on the subject. Later on, you might (and I stress *might*) need a *funding* plan to present to the bank. That's a different matter.

The most important person you need this plan for is yourself and it needn't be a complex document. This is why successful entrepreneurs talk about 'back of an envelope' plans.

think through your financial projections before you leap

But you do need to think through your financial projections before you leap.

Be pessimistic about your projected figures

While you want to be optimistic about most things in your business, when it comes to your figures, put on your miserable hat.

brilliant example

I interviewed a massively successful oil entrepreneur on his approach to risk. His theory is: 'We work out our odds of success in a particular exploration. Then we halve our assumptions of reward, and double our costs. If it still adds up, we go ahead.'

You could do worse than follow his formula.

There are two areas that entrepreneurs tend to miss out on when doing their costings.

Factor in all your indirect costs

Say you are making pottery mugs. There are the obvious costs of the clay and paint. But there are also hidden costs such as the gas to fire them or electricity to run the machines. You might think they are too small to factor in, but as you grow, they can take a big chunk out of your profits.

Cost your own time

One of the biggest oversights people make in start-ups is failing to cost their own time properly. I include myself in this camp. It's easy to do. You are eager and keen, and you don't 'cost' anything. However, this is a real problem when you grow.

Getting trapped

It takes you an hour to make each mug. It takes another hour to pack, deliver, and process payment for each one. You don't care because you are having fun, and you can keep your price down.

Orders flood in. You are suddenly working 60 hours a week. You could employ someone else to do the work, but their hourly rate will be at least £6. Suddenly you are making a loss on each mug. You are trapped.

You need to factor in:

- How much time realistically goes into each item. Include time to purchase your supplies, set-up time, packing and delivery time, and how long it takes to get paid.

- Put in an honest rate for how much you would have to pay *someone else* to do your job. If yours is a specialist skill, don't assume you can get someone for £6 an hour to replace you.

If you charge by the hour, factor in your 'down time'

A mistake service businesses make is to overestimate the number of hours they can work. Say yours is a consultancy business, you might think £20 an hour will give you a good standard of living. Working all day, all week – that's almost £40,000 a year. But you must build in your non-chargeable time. You need to include travel time between jobs, holidays, missed appointments and time off for admin and book-keeping. A more realistic capacity is probably around 65 per cent.

Mojo meter: avoid paralysis by analysis

It's very easy to get bogged down in your figures. You want to keep this step short and sweet. And there is a real risk of disappearing up your own fundament in a misguided attempt to 'plan' out any risk in your business. When you find yourself worrying about the supply source of teaspoons in your café, or you are colour coding the headlines in your plan – you've overdone it.

The problems come out of the woodwork. You start to doubt yourself. This all has *nothing* to do with the viability of your business. It's down to your own self-doubt. It's vital to maintain both your momentum and commitment. If you can't act on your plan now, then put it away and stop thinking about it.

it's vital to maintain both your momentum and commitment

Business is risky – it requires a certain leap into the unknown. Things will change – that's fine, but you've got to be in it to win it.

Let's move on.

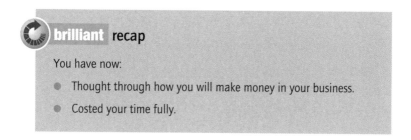

brilliant recap

You have now:

- Thought through how you will make money in your business.
- Costed your time fully.

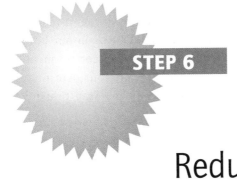

STEP 6

Reduce your start-up costs

'The more up-front money a business requires, the less chance it has of getting off the ground.'

Mark McCormack, *What they don't teach you at Harvard Business School*

You don't need loads of money to start in business. In this step:

1 We reduce your start-up costs.
2 We look for cheap premises.
3 We also take a look at whether e-commerce is a route for you.

Start on the cheap: bootstrapping

brilliant definition

Bootstrapping

Bootstrapping is starting your business with no money.

Shows like 'Dragon's Den', while great for raising the excitement around entrepreneurship, spread a terrible myth: 'To start up, you need loads of money.' It's nonsense.

Bootstrapping is a time-honoured American tradition you'd do well to copy.

brilliant global examples

- Microsoft started off in a garage.
- Google was founded with credit cards.
- Shell Oil started from a small corner shop.

There are many benefits of bootstrapping:

- It saves time trudging around to persuade funders.
- It allows you more time and space to get it wrong.
- You make mistakes on the cheap (trust me, you'll make mistakes). You can then change your strategy without having invested lots of money in the wrong equipment.
- It's a great discipline.

Here's how you do it.

Great bootstrapping techniques

Don't buy anything

It might sound facile, but it's valid. With everything you think you have to buy, think first whether you could rent, lease or borrow it more cheaply. Don't fall into the trap of thinking, 'Well, it's cheaper for me in the long run to buy it.' The most valuable thing for you now is flexibility. By leasing your major purchases, you can update to better equipment quickly and cheaply when the money rolls in, or change quickly if your market is not where you thought it was.

Resist the temptation of what the SAS call 'Shiny Kit Syndrome'. You get so seduced by a piece of beautiful machinery (Satan, take that iPad away from me) that your life will not be complete unless you can clutch it in your hot, sweaty, little hands.

> is it absolutely essential I own it?

Your rule of thumb is not 'Does it gives me the warm fuzzies?' but 'Is it absolutely essential I own it?'

brilliant example

I was asked for advice by a woman starting a business that involved getting people over their fear of flying. Her proposed solution was to build a life-sized flight simulator. Holy moly – that's about £1 million! Surely there's a more creative way to start this without the investment?

Shop around

Everything is negotiable. Always ask for a discount when you buy things, for paying in cash or paying early. The worst they can say is no. See Step 11 for more information on negotiating with suppliers.

Get a deposit

This has to be one of the easiest forms of finance, and yet one people consistently overlook.

Get your clients to pay a deposit for the service, or to pay early.

brilliant example

A designer produced a prototype version of a Christmas card tree (for holding all your cards). She took it to a major retailer who loved it, and ordered 10,000. She then offered them a 10 per cent discount if they would pay a deposit upfront for the order, which they were happy to do. She then used this to pay for her printing.

Offer them a discount for paying in advance. OK, you might lose some profit, but the alternative cost of borrowing could be anything up to 20 per cent.

Build a sense of scarcity. Tell customers there is big demand for your product so they have to pay at least a deposit to guarantee delivery. Bookshops do this with 'advance orders' of popular books, and holiday companies and airlines do it all the time.

Avoid false economies

I'm now going to turn my argument on its head. There are times when you need to buy the most expensive item you can afford.

brilliant example

You need to buy a vehicle for your business. You might be tempted to go for a slightly older model, perhaps saving £500. But then it breaks down. You have £300 in garage fees, it takes up a day of your time (£400), and you lose a new customer (£600). All of a sudden, it's not such a good investment.

brilliant tip

If you buy something often, buy the cheapest. If you buy it once,
buy the most expensive.

Should I work from home?

It's a common question. Many of the largest businesses in the
world were started in bedrooms. Undoubtedly, while you are
researching your market, it makes sense to do this from home.
You don't want to commit yourself to premises until you've
fully researched your idea. But once past this stage, get out!

It can be tempting to carry on working from home, but there
are some real costs:

● Your work tends to spill out into your home life. You find
  yourself nipping off to do a bit of admin or accounts at
  11pm. Your thinking isn't sharp, because you are tired, and
  your business starts to eat up your life.

● You need perspective from your work. Get out as often as
  you can. Even at lunch-time a good walk can clear your
  brain and fire you up.

● The tax implications of working from home aren't great.
  (See Step 13.)

There are alternatives. For example, see if you can sub-let
space in another person's office (perhaps offering your services
as payment-in-kind?).

We were very fortunate in the early days to be offered space in a larger publishers' office. Naturally we expanded round their office like a virus. I knew we had gone too far when I found someone had tied their stapler to their desk with a piece of string.

Don't automatically go for expensive city centre locations. In most instances you will have to visit your clients anyway.

One of my first offices was on a very smart city centre street. However, the space was little more than a collection of glorified broom cupboards with all of us packed in and working off MFI workbenches. When we expanded, we moved to a fairly grotty part of town, but got a lovely, large and trendy open plan office. It's much better for staff morale, excellent for swivel-chair football, there's free car parking, and it costs a fraction of the city centre.

How to pay less for retail property

The following are some ways around the prohibitive cost of premises.

Become a 'destination store'

Even if you are a retail business, you can save money by not going for expensive locations. You do this by becoming a 'destination store'. Offer something exemplary in terms of customer service or sales that people come out of their way to get.

brilliant example

Slaters started as a highly popular Glasgow retailer. They're away from the glitzy main street. However, they gained a reputation for incredible customer service. You are attended to the moment you walk through the door by knowledgeable, friendly and attentive staff. People travelled from far and wide for this service.

When they expanded across the UK, even though they took city centre addresses, they looked for second floor locations to minimise rental costs. They are now one of the top menswear retailers in the UK.

Sub-let space or take a concession

As with sub-letting office space, as a retailer you can also set up as a concession in a larger retailer.

brilliant example

A young sportswear retailer called Tom Hunter spotted a gap in the market for training shoes. He didn't have money for his own store, so approached larger retailers to see if he could take space in their stores. A couple replied. He built up over 30 of these concessions before finally opening his own store, Sports Division. A few years later he sold out for over £250 million.

Avoid signing long leases

Many landlords will try to pressure you into signing 5- or 10- year leases. Avoid long leases like the plague. You won't be able to escape the financial obligation of these even if you cease trading, or move.

avoid long leases like the plague

Don't forget:

- be prepared to negotiate hard
- push to reduce the term
- negotiate easy break-clauses (get a lawyer to check this over)
- watch out for rent reviews which can push your costs up dramatically.

And be prepared to walk away. It's dangerous to become too attached to one spot, and then pay anything to get it. Finally, it's worth paying more for premises that have greater flexibility on lease terms.

Go 'virtual'

The best way to reduce the cost of retail premises is not to have any. The internet offers an excellent way for many stores to set up on the cheap and gives you space and time to refine your offer. A great first step is through eBay. In my work for The Prince's Trust we've seen many businesses set up as eBay businesses. Some of them have now passed the million pound mark. Also, eBay could allow you to sell surplus stock more cheaply without damaging your core price proposition.

This book isn't a definitive guide to e-commerce. But I'll make one observation: build a moat. The internet is a fantastic tool for buyers. You gain access to a multitude of suppliers and can drive the lowest price. But as a vendor, that's not necessarily a good thing. Therefore you want to build a 'defensive moat' to avoid just competing on price. The rules for doing this are the same as for 'bricks and mortar' businesses.

Location

People still have to find you on the web. It's worth investing in your search engine optimisation strategy, and look at building affiliate and referral links to drive traffic to your website.

Don't think you can do this just by advertising. Some dotcoms spent tens of millions on advertising, and still failed to gain enough visitors.

Brand

It helps if your web address is memorable.

brilliant example

www.iwantoneofthose.com. Strapline: 'stuff you really, really want'.

But, as the step on branding points out (page 198), a good brand is as much about reliability as anything else. Even large companies muck this up.

brilliant example

Recently, I booked a flight through a major airline. Halfway through the transaction, the site crashed. How reassuring.

Service

Price is still not the number one factor on the web. I'm not alone in going back to certain more expensive online stores simply because the transaction is simple, they have a transparent returns policy, and they follow up my orders.

price is still not the number one factor on the web

◉ brilliant example

I recently bought a trampoline from Bouncy Happy People. The website was funny, and clear. The process was very simple. They followed up on every stage of the order, and the goods arrived early.

◉ brilliant recap

- You've reduced your start-up costs to as little as possible.
- If you're working from home, you've avoided the pitfalls, and have a plan to get out.
- If you're in an office, you've found a cheaper, though not necessarily central, location.
- If you're in retail, you've tried to become a 'destination' store or looked at sub-letting or concessions as a first stage.
- You've avoided signing a long lease.
- You've seriously considered e-commerce as a way of test trading your main offering or as a subsidiary route to market.
- You've built a 'defensive moat' for your online business.

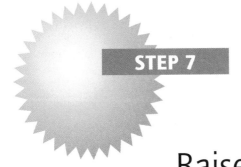

STEP 7

Raise finance

While we've reduced our cash requirements as much as we can, it's still possible we have a funding gap. In this step we look at finance alternatives:

1 We consider personal savings and borrowing.

2 We then look at business angels.

3 We skip quickly over venture capital.

4 We avoid the lure of grants and 'free money'.

5 We see how to raise cash from a bank, particularly in tough times.

6 We pull together a simple funding plan.

Personal savings and borrowing

The most typical finance requirement is for 'working capital', which is often one of the biggest financial hurdles a business can face.

brilliant definition

Working capital

Working capital is the money to keep the wolves from your door in the short term.

Say it takes six months to get your business off the ground before the income comes in. You have a mortgage and perhaps children. Your funding gap could be as much as £12,000. Work out your own 'personal survival budget' – the minimum you need each month to keep your head above water. To do this, keep a track for one month on what you *actually* spend. The problem is that we are too optimistic about how frugal we will be in the future. In reality, money, like socks, has a habit of disappearing inexplicably.

Savings

This is obviously the ideal route, but it can take time to build up this level of savings, especially if you have an idea you are desperate to act on now. If your income reduces substantially, you can sometimes claim a rebate from Her Majesty's Revenue and Customs (HMRC) on tax previously paid. However, this is a longer-term source of cash.

Personal borrowings

It is often easier to borrow money through your personal bank account than it is as a business.

Credit cards

As a method credit cards are very quick and easy: they are also extremely risky. Credit cards are a short-term fix. If you are not paying off balances monthly, they can rack up extremely quickly and interest rates are eye-watering. I avoid personal credit cards and view them as the devil's money.

> credit cards are a short-term fix

Overdrafts

Another comparatively quick and easy source. A personal overdraft is longer term and so should be cheaper than credit cards (so long as it's authorised!).

brilliant example

My room-mate from university, Matt, had a very good relationship with his bank manager. Every holiday, the manager would happily extend his considerable overdraft as Matt passed on stories and photographs of the exotic countries he'd visited. Except the last time Matt returned, the manager had vanished. Evidently so jealous of Matt's stories, he'd chucked in his job to go off travelling!

brilliant tip

Keep your business and personal accounts separate. It's very easy to lump them into one pot, but this will give you poor information on how your business is doing. It can lead to credit problems. It'll be a nightmare when doing your books at year-end, and cause no end of problems with the tax authorities.

Keeping the day job

It's tempting to keep a flow of income while you run the business in your spare time. This is a good idea while you are still in the planning stage. It gives you time to refine your plans, and speak to potential customers. Obviously make sure you are not treading on your current employers' toes if you do this. They're paying you a salary to work for them – just wait until you've got staff and see how you like it!

However, when you are ready to take the plunge, you have to commit full-time. If you are balancing between two lives, you won't give your start-up the attention and time it desperately needs, and it will suffer as a result.

Friends and family

If you have family who are willing to give or lend you money, then you'd be a fool to refuse. My father gave me the money to buy a small car when I started up, and it made a huge difference (thank you!).

A few words of warning before you grab a loan with sticky mitts:

● Only take it for specific purchases. Loose money sloshing around in a business encourages sloppy thinking. Necessity is the mother of invention.

● Be professional. You don't have to draw up expensive agreements, but at least set out what the repayment terms are, what the potential rewards are and what the risks are for the investor if things go wrong.

● Also be aware of the hidden strings attached to 'friendly' money. You don't want dagger looks every time you go to the pub with your mate, or every time you mention a purchase you are making.

As the saying goes 'if you lend money to a friend, be prepared to lose both'.

Business angels

This is Dragon's Den territory. Despite the popularity of the show, this is a less common form of raising finance than you might expect. From the investor's perspective, a minority stake in a small privately-owned business can be next to useless. The business doesn't make a profit because the owners squirrel cash away. Generally, business angels have little control over the decisions and can't sell their stakes.

business angels have little control over the decisions

brilliant definition

Business angel

A business angel is a wealthy person (or a group of people) who is investing for the longer term and taking an equity stake in your business.

While angels are possibly the easiest and 'friendliest' form of outside investment, unless you are setting up a business with substantial new technology or innovation, I wouldn't waste too much time looking for them. If you know a fantastic person you'd love to be involved in your business, try to bring them on as an informal mentor for their advice rather than their money. It'll be worth much more.

> try to bring them on as an informal mentor

Angels will probably want a say in how you run your business. Also, do you really want to give up such a large chunk of your business so early on in the game?

brilliant example

Ian McGlinn ran a small garage. He was approached by a friend who wanted to set up a beauty shop, so he invested £4,000 for a half-share in the company. When his friend, Anita Roddick, ultimately sold her business, The Body Shop, Ian netted around £140 million for his stake.

If this is an appropriate route for you, you can either do it privately through contacts you have or there are also a number of informal angel networking groups (see *Useful contacts*).

Venture capital

Forget it. Unless that is you have a solid industry track record, proven technology and are looking for an investment of £3 million plus.

Grants and the myth of 'free money'

It's a very seductive thought that there's a lot of 'free money' swishing around out there just waiting for you. Don't be seduced.

There is a huge range of government schemes that come and go quite quickly. If you have a sniff around the Enterprise Department of your local council or the Business Link website (see *Useful contacts*) you'll find out whether there's anything relevant to your specific circumstances.

As a taxpayer, you'd be alarmed that people are making off with your cash. And there's the rub. There is so much paperwork involved in this process it can take forever.

brilliant example

I was involved in helping a free newspaper get off the ground. One of the directors spent six months of his start-up applying for grants. They had to change their legal structure, take a range of people onto the board and fill out endless forms. By the time they got the money, they didn't need it.

If they'd invested all that time and effort into selling to advertisers, they would have got the money much quicker.

Innovation grants

The exception is if you have a high-tech business with a high degree of product innovation. There are several technology grant schemes listed on the Business Link website (**www. businesslink.gov.uk**) and the Scottish Enterprise website (**www.scottish-enterprise.com**), such as the Proof of Concept scheme to name a specific example.

Support 'in-kind'

Forgetting the cash, there's a lot of other non-financial assistance available from government agencies. This can be worth much more. Examples include:

- training courses (either free or substantially discounted)
- help finding staff, and funding assistance
- discounted places on foreign trade missions and help in exporting
- technology support
- help registering patents and trade marks.

You should tap into this network as soon as you start your business plans through your Business Link in England or Local Enterprise Company in Scotland.

The Prince's Trust/Prince's Scottish Youth Business Trust

If you are aged 14–30 (or 18–25 in Scotland), there is one door you should definitely be knocking on. The Prince's Trust/ Prince's Scottish Youth Business Trust (see *Useful contacts*) is a charity to help young people starting in business. It provides support in a wide range of ways:

- Finance and soft loans. It can give you very low interest rate loans up to £5,000, and in special circumstances, grants.
- Mentoring. It will coach you through the process of getting your business ready. You then go before a friendly panel to discuss your ideas. If you get the money, you then get an experienced business person to act as your mentor.
- Training. You get courses such as book-keeping, start-up guides and networking events.

I got my start-up money from the charity and have been a big fan ever since.

Raising cash from a bank

The reality of small business banking

As a small business, you have to realise how little you are worth, financially, to a bank. We have the lowest level of bank charges in Europe, but this comes at a price.

Don't expect your bank manager to be there, holding your hand and helping you make decisions. For a start, they are not allowed to give you advice. And they don't have the time. Small business banking is often now dealt with through the 'retail' division of a bank. This means they treat you in much the same way as you get treated as a personal customer, so don't expect a close personal relationship service.

keep to your agreed limits

Keep to your agreed limits. As with personal accounts, the free banking service is often subsidised by high charges for those who go beyond borrowing limits.

Hazard

Beware of 'personal guarantees' – you could lose your home.

Often when you are looking to borrow start-up money or get a business overdraft from a bank it will ask you for a personal guarantee. Often this will mean putting your property as security. After all, you have zero trading history as a business. You can try and negotiate your way out of this completely, but in most cases the bank will want something.

However, do make sure you negotiate a time limit on this guarantee. You might be able to get this down to six months, which is pretty reasonable. Be prepared to shop around on this point. If you give an unlimited guarantee, you are permanently at risk of losing your house if your business goes under. Sometimes things can get ridiculous.

brilliant example

Our bank account has maintained a six-figure credit balance for many years. We asked our bank for an extra credit card for a director with a couple of grand limit. It said it would, but I would have to put my house up as security. I could have done, but the principle of the matter made me tell them where to stick it.

Shop around

Banks usually have a 'traffic light' system of how they view risk from different industries. The view changes from month to month, and they will be loath to tell you what their view is of your particular sector at any one time. This might mean that different banks

it can pay to shop around

might view your business proposition differently, depending on what their view of the sector is, so it can pay to shop around.

This also applies to other products the bank might want to cross-sell. You don't have to have all your financial products with one provider. It may seem more convenient, but this can come at a price. You can usually get better prices on your business insurance, credit cards, pension and savings from alternative providers to your main bank.

Different sources of money from banks

Banks are large complex beasts, and often one arm doesn't know what the other arm is up to. I've heard of people trying to borrow money as a business loan, and being made to jump over all sorts of hurdles and not getting it. In the same breath they've asked to extend the overdraft for the same amount, and got it immediately.

So, in addition to a straightforward loan, consider other sources of borrowing:

1 *Asset finance.* If you need considerable amounts of equipment in your business, do you need to actually own it? Asset finance can be used to purchase all kinds of equipment and machinery. You can also use it to fund vehicles and computer equipment. The great advantage is that by paying a monthly sum, you don't have to tie up all your start-up cash in a series of assets.

2 *Invoice finance.* As we cover in Step 12 on cashflow, this is a way to bridge a gap in your funding. Simply, your invoice finance provider will pay you a proportion of your invoice soon after you issue it. This should reduce your working capital needs while you wait to get paid.

Post credit crunch finance

Since the first edition of this book, the biggest impact on business has probably been the bank bust and resultant 'credit crunch'.

Down-turn start-ups

The fall-out from this has led to a fairly long-running recession. I'm not going to say much about this. For a start, as small business people, there's nothing we can do about it except be optimistic and keep going. I also think a down-turn is one of the best times to start up.

To begin with, competitors get shaken out of the market. They might also have higher costs than your nimble operation, giving you a real edge. It also means your costs can be much lower – rents on property, suppliers desperate for your business, and access to staff you might not be able to afford in boom times.

Setting up in a down-turn also makes your business fantastically robust. You have to tempt cash-strapped customers, you need to pare your costs to the bone and operate with lean and mean efficiency. This discipline will stand you in wonderful stead when the up-turn comes. Far better than being a bloated boomtime business.

> this discipline will stand you in wonderful stead

Raising finance post-crunch

However, one downside is the availability of finance for start-ups. Caught out in the up-swing, banks are holding tight to their cash. While I'll always be an advocate for frugal borrowing, there are some times where it's unavoidable. So here's some guidance on how to raise cash in tight times.

How to convince a bank to lend

The same rules apply as in good times, but now they are essential. Minimise the risk. Shop around.

1 UK banks have produced a checklist to support customers. You can ask your bank for this, or you can get a copy from **www.betterbusinessfinance.co.uk**.

2 Be clear about the finance you need: state the exact amount you need, the valid business purpose you need it for, and the term over which you plan to repay the money.

3 Then you have to minimise the bank's perception of risk for you. There are a number of ways to do this:

- Financial: show them previous trading statements (if you have them). Detail the assets you or your business have and any security you can provide against the lending. In good times, it's possible to get away with minimal security, but that's far harder when cash is tight.

- You also need to convince them about your plans. Detail your background and all the relevant experience you have. Share your research. Come armed with a stack of pre-orders or letters of recommendation from potential customers. Anything that reassures you're a sure thing.

If the bank rejects your application, don't forget that you have a right to appeal this decision. These appeals are now scrutinised by an independent assessor on behalf of the government, so the banks will take this process seriously.

While the process varies from bank to bank, the principles are set out at the website above.

As a note of caution however, don't just get into this process because you feel miffed. You can waste a huge amount of time just to repair your sense of pride. Only follow this route if you're pretty sure there has been a clear error in the decision process.

Alternative sources of funding

In response to great campaigning by small business organisations, the government is putting cash behind a number of funding sources. You might want to consider these.

Enterprise Finance Guarantee (EFG)

Probably the best of the bunch for small businesses is the EFG. It's been in existence for a number of years as the Small Firms Loan Guarantee Scheme. It supports lending by offering the banks an additional guarantee against 75 per cent of a loan to a small business. It's ideal for businesses with strong growth potential but a varied credit history, or lack of security (i.e. almost every small business!).

In the past, banks were strangely reluctant to mention this to new customers, so it's something you actively have to ask about. The government's business department (**www.bis.gov. uk**) has details, as do most banks.

The Business Growth Fund

You might have read the headlines about this £2.5 billion fund, set up by the big banks on the government's orders. Unfortunately for start-ups, it's aimed at enterprises with a turnover above £10 million. You can learn more at their website (**www.businessgrowthfund.co.uk**).

European Investment Bank

The Europeans have also got in on the act. This fund is available through mainstream banks. It offers discounted rates and higher protection for banks. You cannot borrow for working capital, but only to invest in capital expenditure.

How to pitch for funding

If you need finance, you are going to have to sell your proposition to the bank/funder. Many of the rules of selling apply here (and are covered in Step 9), but there are some additional points about financing.

Your business plan 'pitch' for funding

We've already covered the importance of having your own plan and view of the business: this is different. What we need now is a sales document, and you should approach it as such. It's not a place to explore potential options; it's a place to present certainties and facts. If you don't need to raise finance, you don't need one. If you only need a small amount of money and you have security, then you might only need a couple of pages along with your figures. Banks often have their own templates, and it can be a good idea to follow these so it looks familiar to them.

These are the main things you'll want to consider in your 'pitch' document.

People buy people

Ultimately, the funder is buying you, not the business. They are betting on your ability to make it happen. I'm afraid to say, first impressions *do* count. An experienced interviewer from a leading company once told me she usually decided on a candidate 30 seconds after they had walked in the door.

first impressions *do* count

You want to inspire confidence. This doesn't mean being cocky and arrogant. Be yourself, but look after the little things: dress smart, look them in the eye when you walk in, smile and shake hands. Make sure you know the details of your plan and have all the relevant paperwork and examples to hand.

Put lots of your own relevant personal experience in the plan. The key is relevance to your business. No-one cares about your Geography O-Level I'm afraid. Also put in other team members, support network and mentors/advisers you have in your 'dream team'.

Reassure on your revenue assumptions

The biggest grey area for a funder is whether your financial predictions are reliable. This is where you talk through your sales assumptions and the strong research you have to support them. Talk through your experiences, customer comments, orders and testimonials.

Funders love 'letters of intent'. Even if someone hasn't bought something, a short letter saying that they are very likely to when you start up is very reassuring.

Include some 'stress testing' on your figures. That way, funders can be reassured that even if your sales are 20 per cent lower than anticipated, or costs 20 per cent higher (which by the way, is extremely likely!) then you still have a viable business. It also shows you've thought things through.

Show your commitment

If you can prove your personal investment in making something work, a funder will be reassured. The most obvious is how much of your own money you've put in. Usually a funder will expect you to match their funding commitment. But it can also include personal statements about your commitment over the long term.

How to handle questions and objections

The greatest plan can fail if you don't pitch it well. The following are some pointers to handling questions.

There is a secret rule of interviews, and one you'll see politicians using all the time: answer the question you want, and not necessarily the one you've been asked. You need to prepare a list of the strengths of your plan in advance, and look for ways to bring this in throughout the interview.

> the greatest plan can fail if you don't pitch it well

brilliant example

Potential funders will ask you what your experience in running a restaurant has been. You've never done it before. So instead, you talk about your experience of working in a restaurant, and all the areas that covered, then you bring in the experience of your team (including a prominent restaurateur as mentor), then you move on to your revenue assumptions and how realistic these are.

If you are asked a question you don't understand, or don't have an answer to – ask for more clarification. If you still honestly don't know the answer, don't get flustered or lie. It's far better to say, 'I'm sorry, I don't have the information to hand at the moment. Is it OK if I get back to you shortly with that?'

Don't get into an argument. If they raise an objection you don't agree with, start by acknowledging their concern, then deflect it with evidence you have.

brilliant example

Interviewer	I don't think there's space for another restaurant in the high street.
Bad reply	Well, there is. You're wrong I'm afraid.
Good reply	It's interesting you should say that. A number of other people have said that to us when we first presented our ideas. However, what we found when we did our research was that there is a specific niche in the market that is currently not being served. Let me talk through our findings around this...

What your plan should contain

1 Brief summary of your idea.

- What the market is: show the market demand. How can your prove this?

- Why your idea is unique. What is the gap in the market you are looking to serve?

- Forecasted profits. Longer-term prospects. How much finance is required.

2 You and your team.

- Track record with key achievements for yourself.

- Other people who will be helping you: they don't have to be employed, they can be mentors and supporters.
- An honest appreciation of your strengths and weaknesses, and what you will do to bridge these.

3   Your product or service.

- A brief description of what it is and what needs it is servicing.
- Your target market (current size and your predictions on growth). Put the main points here and keep any detailed supporting statistics in the appendix.
- A more detailed analysis of the specific niche your product/service will fit.
- Your competitors: who are the prime ones and how will you compete against them?
- What are the unique selling points of your product/service?
- A SWOT analysis: your Strengths, Weaknesses, Opportunities and Threats.

4   Sales and marketing.

- Your price, and how you decided on this.
- Place: where will you be selling your product from?
- Who will do the selling?
- What promotional plans you have.

5   Operations management.

- Suppliers.
- Equipment needed.

6   Financials.

- Your forecasts, and the *evidence* behind your assumptions.
- Monthly cashflow forecast for year one, and quarterly for year two.
- Profit and loss forecast.
- Balance sheet.

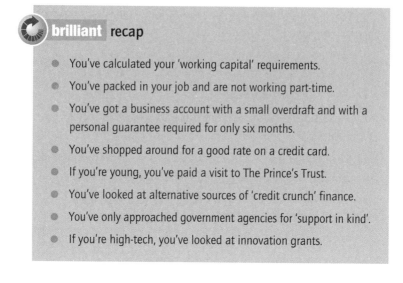

brilliant recap

- You've calculated your 'working capital' requirements.
- You've packed in your job and are not working part-time.
- You've got a business account with a small overdraft and with a personal guarantee required for only six months.
- You've shopped around for a good rate on a credit card.
- If you're young, you've paid a visit to The Prince's Trust.
- You've looked at alternative sources of 'credit crunch' finance.
- You've only approached government agencies for 'support in kind'.
- If you're high-tech, you've looked at innovation grants.

STEP 8

Take care of
the small print

In this step, we look at the legal requirements in starting up. This is an intentionally short chapter. It's a misconception that there are onerous hurdles to overcome in starting up. We look at:

1 Whether to become a 'limited' business.
2 Who else you have to register with.
3 Simple business insurance.

Decide whether you should be a 'limited company'

You'll see many businesses are described as 'limited'. The original principle behind this was to encourage more people to start up businesses by limiting their personal liability for any debts if their business should fail. At first sight, that looks like a 'no-brainer' – it sounds like the perfect insurance policy. Well, it's not so simple. Not surprisingly, the reward comes with a number of additional responsibilities.

It requires more paperwork

Your company must be registered at Companies House (**www. companieshouse.gov.uk**). To do this, you must complete the following documents:

- Memorandum of Association, which includes your company name, location and type of business. Note that registering the name of your company does not mean it becomes a registered trade mark, and that no-one else can use it.

- Articles of Association, which outlines directors' powers, shareholder rights and so on. You don't have to create these from scratch. Standard ones can be purchased from stationers for around £20–£30.

You'll then need to sign:

- Form 10: this gives directors' names and private home addresses, together with your registered company address.

- Form 12: this states that the company complies with the terms of the Companies Act. Each year, you must have your annual accounts audited, and file these and an annual return at Companies House. As a small company, you can file 'abbreviated accounts'. This isn't a particularly expensive or difficult process. It does, however, mean anyone can access your basic figures to see how your company is doing. You have nine months to pay corporation tax after your year end.

The tax position is different

A company must pay corporation tax on any profits it makes. On top of this, you as a director must pay income tax and national insurance on your pay as an 'employee' of the company. This may seem like a double whammy, but bear in mind that the alternative as a sole trader is to be taxed on your business's profits on an individual salary basis. So any profit you make that takes you into the higher rate tax bands you'll be taxed at a hefty 40 or 50 per cent. This compares with the lower corporation tax rate (called the small profits rate) of 20 per cent for profits of up to £300,000. You can also pay yourself and any other directors a dividend (or number of dividends throughout the year) from the profits of the company. Again, the tax rate on this is lower than the higher rate of personal income tax.

As you can see, the tax issues around this can be tricky. If tax is likely to be a major issue for you, then it's a good idea to speak to an accountant to find out what option best suits your circumstances.

You can issue shares

One attraction of a limited company is that you can give or sell shares to other participants. You cannot do this as a sole trader.

You might not escape your liabilities

Not surprisingly, banks and funders are worried about people skipping away from their debts. Most will therefore require some additional form of personal guarantee against any loans or overdrafts they make to the business. Therefore, you might find you've been the whole way through the incorporation process to find the bank requires its loan to you to be secured against your home. (For advice about avoiding this, see Step 7.)

As a director, there are certain standards you have to comply with (such as not continuing to trade when you know you are insolvent). Failure to comply can result in legal action.

The alternatives

Sole trader

This is the simplest way to start in business and requires little or no paperwork. If you are not forming a company, then you are counted as 'self-employed' and must register as such with HMRC. It has a Newly Self-Employed Helpline on 0845 915 4515.

You have to make an annual self-assessment tax return to HMRC. You must also keep records showing your business income and expenses. You will normally have until the end of January to complete your tax return or be liable for a fine starting at £100.

Many people have the mistaken view that you should automatically be a limited company as it's more 'professional'. Don't fall for the snobbery. After all, the department store chain John Lewis isn't a limited company, and it's certainly not done it any harm!

Partnership

A partnership is a relatively simple way for two or more people to start in business together. However, you are not creating a distinct company, so you are both ostensibly still self-employed, and the tax treatment is the same. You have also not limited your liability from any debts the business might run up.

There is a slight distinction between the legal treatment of debts in Scotland and with the rest of the UK. In Scotland, you are 'severally' liable, which means one partner is not responsible for the total debts of the partnership. In the rest of the UK, you cannot 'sever' this liability, which means each partner is responsible for the total debts of the business – even if they have not been taken out in their name.

In Step 4 I cautioned you about the risks of setting up in partnership just because you feel lonely. If however it is right for you, then draw up a detailed partnership agreement at the outset. This should cover all the areas you will have responsibility for, how you will make decisions if the two of you don't agree (often by relying on an impartial third party you both trust) and how you will dissolve the partnership if your individual priorities change.

> draw up a detailed partnership agreement at the outset

Far too many partnerships fail to do this, probably because they feel it's bad luck at the outset – a bit like asking for a 'pre-nup' before getting married. Don't duck the issue. Do it, then file it in a bottom drawer where you'll (hopefully) never look at it again.

Who else do I have to register with?

Your tax status is likely to change, so you'll need to notify HMRC. If your turnover hits a certain level, you'll have to register for VAT (see Step 13). Depending on your specific industry sector, there might be additional health and safety rules to comply with. To check these out, visit **www.hmrc. gov.uk/factsheet/working-for-yourself.pdf**.

That's pretty much it. I told you I'd keep it simple!

Get appropriate insurance

Hazard

Don't let a falling tree put you out of business.

A simple accident at the wrong time can put your business off the road. It seems like an avoidable cost, but insurance can be essential for your new business.

brilliant example

Starting from a kitchen table, Abel Eastern had grown to corner the market in supplying nan breads to UK supermarkets. At about 3am one night, a fire broke out in its main factory. Only its insurance had run out at midnight. The company had not reinsured as it was in a dispute with the broker. By the time it gathered the funds to rebuild the business, competition had moved in and hoovered up its client base.

However, don't go overboard, but be smart about the insurances you buy:

- It's a false economy not getting insurance, particularly if it's for an essential piece of kit, such as a van. Go through an insurance broker to get the best price and policy for you. Don't necessarily go for the cheapest; look for fast payout and minimal hassle.

- Be careful what you insure. Generally, if the risk is very expensive, then you should insure it (e.g. expensive kit, your life). However, if the cost of the risk is relatively small, then it's often a waste of money insuring it (e.g. your mobile phone/laptop). In particular, avoid the add-on protection sale that many electrical retailers will hit you with. It's where they make an eye-watering amount of their profit. If you are going to insure something always shop around.

- Weigh up whether a financial payout is going to solve your problems. In our business, I'm frequently prompted by sales people to buy 'key person' insurance. This would pay me a lump sum if a key member of staff becomes long-term sick. The premiums are quite high. In my view, if one of our great designers falls sick, then it will take a considerable amount of time and effort to replace them. But having a lump sum payment from an insurer is not going to make that process any quicker or easier.

Other insurances

Employers' liability compulsory insurance (ELCI)

If you employ staff, you need compulsory insurance against your staff being injured. It's not hugely expensive, and is certainly not a reason to put off employing staff. Shop around for the cheapest deal.

Public liability

If members of the public come onto your premises, you might want to insure yourself against their injury (depending on how likely this is). This is slightly more complex than ELCI, and it's worth speaking to a broker.

Professional indemnity insurance

If you sell your knowledge or skill, then you can be liable for actions your clients take on your advice. Most 'professionals' hold some form of this cover. It can be fairly expensive, but you can reduce it by documenting your quality check systems and showing these to insurers.

brilliant recap

By now you should have:

- Decided whether it's right to be a limited company or not.
- Notified HMRC about your changed tax status.
- Checked any sector specific health and safety regulations.
- Insured only your most important assets.

Congratulations, you're now ready to trade!

PHASE 2

Into action

In this phase, we launch our businesses.

Step 9 Get selling

Step 10 Set your price

Step 11 Now, make your product/service

Step 12 Get the cash in

Step 13 Do your books

Step 14 Do a quick risk audit

STEP 9

Get selling

It's time for the most important start-up stage: sales. In this, the longest step in the book:

1 We look at how to get yourself mentally prepared.
2 We work through 20 golden sales techniques.
3 Sadly, we see how getting someone else to do it for you isn't an option for the start-up.

Why selling matters

Sales is the single most important task for you. A flow of sales can cover a multitude of sins. You can have mediocre products, haphazard service, a lack of staff, and still succeed. Conversely, I've met businesses with the most amazing technology in the world, but without the proper sales approach, they've got nowhere.

But sales is more than flogging things to unsuspecting punters. It's being out there in the market every day, listening to customers, adjusting your offering and comparing it with competitors. If you're stuck in your nice warm office, colour-coding your accounts and framing your motivational posters, you are not going to get anywhere.

When I evaluate a business, I put the plan aside and weigh up the person: 'Do they have the willingness to step outside their comfort zone and get out talking to customers?' If not, then I won't back the business.

You should be spending at least 50 per cent of your time out speaking to people. This is a stiff target, and you'll be lucky if it's 15 per cent, but keep it in mind.

I'm sorry if you don't like the advice. I know many people would rather eat a pair of leather shoes than make a cold sales call. That's why I'm going to make it as easy as I can for you.

How to prepare yourself mentally

Why sales are so hard and how to get over it

There is one unavoidable fact in sales: you are going to get dumped – frequently. Sales is largely a numbers game. No matter how brilliant your proposition, it won't be right for many people. The secret of sales? Learn not to take this rejection personally.

It's all down to basic human psychology. I actually did a psychology degree at university, but I have to admit the following is borrowed more from *Cosmopolitan* magazine than the annals of the British Psychological Society. Fundamentally, we are social animals. We all want to be liked and approved of. We take at least half (and often more) of our sense of self-worth from what others around us tell us. Therefore, if your business is dear to your heart, and you get three people a day saying they don't want it, pretty soon you'll feel you are a worthless person and want to crawl under the duvet.

fundamentally, we are social animals

The following is designed to lessen the pain.

'It's not you, it's me...' Why people say no

There's no getting away from it: rejection hurts.

brilliant example

Having been at an all-boys school all my childhood, I was understandably excited at my first date, aged 13, with Debbie. It was a double date with my best friend Paul, and while he got smoochy on the ghost train, Debbie and I held hands.

I was hooked. I spent all that night sleeplessly thinking of valiant scenarios where I would rescue Debbie.

The following day we all went for a bike ride. She dumped me. Then I got a flat tyre. And it started raining.

Took me, ooooo, about 10 months to get over it.

There is a bit of valid psychology called Agency Theory. Basically, if you are closely involved in a situation (say an accident), you automatically over-emphasise the role of the people involved – the principal agents. However, when speaking to independent witnesses, they have a much more balanced view of what happened, which includes externals such as weather, road conditions, etc.

It's the same in selling. If things go wrong, we over-blame ourselves (how was I to know Debbie had secretly fancied my friend for months?). There are actually a range of other factors you've probably not considered.

Timing

I've always thought it more important to be Mr Right Now than Mr Right. Successful sales is often just being in the right place at the right time. It's also why I need to introduce you to a lady called AIDA. This simple piece of marketing theory explains the buying process your customers will typically go through: Awareness, Interest, Desire, Action – AIDA.

- The first time someone hears about your business, they have **A**wareness. They're not ready to buy.

- The second time they hear about it, it might have heightened to **I**nterest (or, better yet, they are **I**ntrigued). They are still not buying though.

- The third time they hear, they might have actual **D**esire for your product or service. Almost there!

- But only on the fourth contact will they finally take any **A**ction.

Some people add a fifth stage before Action of 'Convincing'. It's probably right, but it messes up my nice acronym so I've ignored it.

This translates into a startling fact:

80 per cent of sales come after the fourth contact you make with a prospect.

The important thing is that you keep plugging away at your sales prospects. Don't automatically try to close the sale on your first contact. But also don't give up if they don't bite first time.

> don't give up if they don't bite first time

This process also applies to marketing (of which more in Step 16).

Many start-ups make the mistake of putting a massive amount of money into a single piece of marketing, such as a leaflet or a press advert. Then they sit back to wait for the customers to roll in. The mail shot might have done a great job at 'awareness' or even 'interest', but to close the sale (get any 'action'), you're going to have to knock on that door yourself.

Work out your 'snog to slap' ratio

As any Casanova at your local nightclub will tell you, you've got to get your face slapped a few times.

Now I think about it, my mate Paul also snogged the second girl I fancied, Carol. I'd fancied her from afar for years but not said anything. Paul came to stay for the weekend and before I knew it, the two of them were getting smoochy – again!

I couldn't believe it. I asked Paul his secret. After all, he looks like a gorilla. He said, 'I ask.' That's the difference. It doesn't matter if some say no, sooner or later you'll get a yes or two. But you won't if you never ask.

My hit rate is seven. It takes me seven calls before I get through to someone. Of these connections, one in seven will turn into a lead. Of these seven, one will convert into a sale. So from now on in life, if I'm pitching anything to anyone, I always make sure I have a minimum of seven alternatives.

I don't believe I am uniquely rubbish as a sales person, it's just the way of the world. The secret is to always have options up your sleeve, and not fret about the no's – they all take you closer to the yes. The faster you can get through them, the better.

Get a sales funnel

Sales professionals talk about their 'sales funnel'. This is a pool of prospects and different stages of sale. An entrepreneur I knew used to describe this as a barrel filled with water. So long as he kept adding to it, it would overflow a little bit at a time.

So your job in sales is not always to be winning work, but it is to be moving people down your sales funnel. Work out what your ratio of calls is, then set this as your weekly call target.

You'll be amazed that after a week of getting nowhere, the phone will ring with a client calling you (it does happen!), or someone says, 'It's just what I'm looking for, how on earth did you know to call me today?' At which point you just nod enigmatically and try not to burst into tears of relief.

How to keep your self-esteem topped up

So, even though you know it's a numbers game, and not to take rejection personally, this is still usually the toughest stage of business. The following can help.

Grasp the nettle

If you hate sales, there's no point putting it off. Lump all your calls together, and get it out of the way as soon as you can. Perhaps start with a warmer lead – someone you know who might give you the time of day (and no, your mum doesn't count). Then you'll find the other calls flow more easily.

lump all your calls together

Care less about your business

I read recently about the strong similarities between highly successful business leaders and sociopaths.

It's certainly very hard to sell when you care passionately about what you are selling. If customers don't get it, you have to resist the urge to lean across the table, grab their lapels and shake them vigorously until they see your point. So, it helps to put some distance between what you are selling and yourself. If you are a crafts person, try to sell 'packages' of what you make, or think of yourself on certain days of the week as just the sales rep for your business.

Know when to change tack

I was speaking to a young guy who'd set up a student newspaper. He'd made over 100 cold calls to advertisers and they'd all said 'no'.

There comes a point when banging your head against a brick wall when you realise you are only going to get a headache. If your sales are really going nowhere after 30 or 40 calls, you probably need to go back to look at your proposition.

Think laterally about distribution

Getting a major retailer to stock your product can be a thankless task. You often find yourself stuck in a Catch-22 where they'll only stock successful selling products, yet you can't build that track record.

Perhaps it's time to try to approach the block from a different angle.

brilliant global example

Richard Tait knew his board game would sell. The problem was convincing the major US toy retailers to back his hunch. But as he sat sipping his café latte in a Starbucks, he hit on a novel solution. He noticed his target customers were all around him. So he convinced the coffee chain to trial selling his board game as something different for customers. Word spread, and sales rocketed. Tait's game, 'Cranium', became the fastest selling board game in history.

Mojo meter: reward yourself

You've done all this hard work, and it's starting to pay off. It's time to reward yourself. We're simple creatures, and respond to simple rewards.

The beauty of having a ratio and target is that once you've hit it, you can have a break and bathe in a warm feeling of smug self-satisfaction. You've hit your target for the day: give yourself the rest of the day off! You've hit your sales target for the month: give yourself a week's holiday! Or you've won a new piece of lucrative work: give yourself a sales bonus. Even when it's your own business, knowing one call might give you £500, which could pay for a short holiday, is one hell of an incentive (remember to account for the tax on this!).

I used to buy myself electronic gadgets after landing big sales. What a saddo.

'I don't have to sell, my customers come to me'

Lucky you, but I don't think you get off the hook quite so easily. It's the difference between a 'normal' shop where someone skulks behind the counter, and a 'brilliant' one where they come out and engage you in friendly conversation. Don't lurk behind your sales proposition, whatever it is – it is extremely off-putting.

One entrepreneur I know would always stand in front of his stall, looking quizzical. Customers were happy to stand next to him and look the same way. He could then casually engage them in conversation, before leading them in for the kill (not literally you understand).

Have a series of conversation openers and talking points ready. The Queen always asks, 'Have you come far?'

brilliant example

A Scottish oil engineer would take stands at foreign trade shows. His great idea was to have a model oil rig built with a timer inside it. Every hour, to a big fanfare, he would get a 'gusher' and whisky would come shooting out the top of his rig. It was a huge talking point, and a fantastic sales tool.

20 golden sales techniques

Start close to home

The wrong way to sell is the 'shotgun' approach: 'everyone is a potential customer for me'.

Instead, take a 'sniper' approach. Start with your easiest to win customers, people who trust or know you, and work outwards from there.

Approach your competitors' clients and get them to switch. I know it sounds unfair, but this is business. You know they have the budgets, and they're in the market for your product and service. You just have to make your offering better.

Understand what the customer really wants to buy

Hopefully you've taken this on board from Step 3 on research. But don't forget the difference it makes in sales.

---

brilliant example

A number of big consortiums were bidding for the right to run the Lottery. Most of them went in on the amounts of money they could raise, and their whizzy marketing ideas. The Camelot consortium looked harder at the 'buyers'. They were civil servants. There was no benefit for them in making this a massive success; they just wanted to keep their jobs. The thrust of Camelot's pitch therefore was 'safe pair of hands'. All they talked about was not cocking things up. They won.

Be enthusiastic!

People buy people. If you are passionate and enthusiastic about your idea, it will rub off. Customers will be buying you as much as the product or service. You'd be amazed at how much of a difference this makes. And it doesn't matter how serious the audience is.

Be a doctor not a sales person

Customers are understandably wary of pushy sales people. Instead, you want to come across as an expert, a consultant, a doctor. Look at your job description. Don't call yourself 'sales director', but 'antiques expert'.

Involve your customer

brilliant example

We were looking for a new bathroom. A 'design consultant' came to see us. She had some snazzy software on her laptop. We sat together, we planned where things would go, and what colour the tiles would be, etc. She didn't have to sell a thing, we sold ourselves.

Ask open questions

You want to get your customers to open up about their needs. To do this, you need to ask 'open-ended' questions to get them talking. 'Closed' questions can be answered with just yes or no, and so end your meeting.

Bad closed questions	Good open questions
Have you ever thought about...? ('No')	**What are** your main objectives?
How many products do you have? ('Six')	**Why** do you focus on this?
Do you buy from sales people? ('No, goodbye')	**How do** you choose a supplier?

Go in with a referral

If you mention the right person's name, you can jump three stages of trust in one go. How do you get them? Ask. At the end of every call and meeting, ask 'Who else do you know who might be interested?' They'll often give you names to get you off the phone or out of their living room. If you do this to 10 people, and they each give you three names, you'll have 30 excellent leads. And it grows exponentially from there.

Write out a good sales script

I always work through what I'm going to ask in a sales call, and what my objective is. Then I chuck it in the bin. You want to be 'natural' in a meeting, but often being effortless takes a huge amount of preparation.

Think through possible objections in advance

Objections are good so learn to love them. They show the customer is considering buying. If you can answer them all, then you have the sale. Just don't fold at the first one.

> objections are good so learn to love them

The following are the three most common objections, and how to get round them:

1 Loyalty to an existing supplier.

2 Lack of perceived demand.

3 Price.

The following shows how to handle them.

The customer says	What they mean	What you do
'I'm happy with my current supplier'	Loyalty	1 Don't slag the competition – you will undermine the person you are selling to.
		2 Ask lots of questions about the competitor's service/ product.
		3 Stress the difference of your offer.
		4 Get the customer to consider a trial offer.
'I can't see me needing that'	Demand	1 Actively question them about why not.
		2 Talk through your current customer base and why they use you.
		3 Come back to them.
'It's too expensive	Price	1 Question the client – 'What makes you say that?'
		2 Get a comparison with other products.
		3 Question the customer on the benefits you offer and their need.
		4 Stress the value you add and not the cost.

Don't go overboard with answers, and dig yourself into a hole. Answer succinctly and learn to shut up.

When someone comes up with an objection, stifle your urge to say: 'No, don't be a fool!' Nod sagely and say: 'It's interesting you should say that, but what we found in fact was...' You can never win an argument with a prospective customer, but you can gently change their point of view.

Often you'll find new customers are interested in your product or service, but are nervous about experimenting with it. Why not give them the chance to sample?

---

brilliant global example

The founders of French start-up WineSide had noticed people were keen to experiment with new wines, but nervous about spending large sums on something they might not like. So the company retails 10cl sealed tubes of Grand Cru wines so its customers can experiment without breaking the bank. It now extends this to restaurants so they can offer high-quality wines by the glass without having to open a whole bottle.

Be courteous

You must know the telesales people who'll carry on with their sales spiel even after you've chopped their heads off. You don't have to be like that. It's amazing what a little courteousness will do at the start of a call. Always ask, 'Do you have a couple of moments?' Most often people will say, 'So long as you're quick.' If they say they're really busy, then you can get a good time to call back.

Only ask a question to which the most likely answer is 'yes'

'Am I interrupting you?' you politely ask. 'Of course you bloody are! Did you think I was waiting for your call?' Also try to get the customer to say 'yes' to at least three things early in your pitch. It brings them onto your side.

Make sure you are speaking to the decision maker

Or as a friend used to say more bluntly: 'Make sure you're speaking to the organ grinder and not the monkey.' It's a mistake I've made far too many times. The person might not be the actual decision maker. Holidays, cars, major purchases: it's my wife.

In a sales meeting, ignore the 'noddies'. It's so easy to speak to the person doing all the nodding and seeming really friendly. That means nothing I'm afraid, other than they're possibly a bit simple. Quite often it's the quiet, grumpy-looking one you have to influence.

On the flip side, many female entrepreneurs I've met talk about being ignored in supplier meetings while the sales person addresses the man. If that happens to you, play it to your advantage. People are more likely to be off-guard if they underestimate you, and it can be a great bargaining tool.

Don't automatically aim high

You want to sell something to a large company. It's a mistake to aim at the top of the ladder: it's impossible to get hold of them. Quite often decisions are made at a far lower level by people who are overlooked. Also, it's these people who your relationship is with. People don't want solutions imposed from 'on high' and will do everything in their power to kick you out if they didn't get to hire you in the first place.

> people don't want solutions imposed from 'on high'

Bait the hook

Your sales calls will be much more effective if you have something of value to offer to the recipient.

Don't say   Can I come to show you our products?

Do say   I'd like to show how other people in your industry have been able to save 8 per cent on their costs.

Find the best time to sell

There is no hard and fast rule for this: it depends on your customers. If you are calling a business, the middle of the morning or afternoon can be bad times as people will be stuck into projects. First thing in the morning, just after lunch, or close to the end of the day can be good. Similarly, I've often found Friday afternoon is a good time to call, as people have that 'Thank Crunchie it's Friday' feeling and are more tolerant to my ham-fisted sales pitch.

Keep a note of your call rates, and see when works best.

Get through the gate keeper

Receptionists, secretaries, PAs: the further up the tree you are going, the more blockers there are going to be. Their role is to keep sales people like us away from their superiors. (I once even had someone put on a funny voice so they could pretend not to be in.)

brilliant tips

1   The best way past blockers is with a referral. Get the name of anyone else in their department and say, 'Bob suggested I speak to them.'

2   Suggest you are already in a dialogue: 'It's a follow-up call.'

3   Just give out your first name.

4   Don't fall for: 'I'll ask them to call you back.' No, they won't.

5   Call the press office. They're usually friendly types not afraid of the phone, and will put you through.

Stand and smile

Make your phone calls standing up and smiling. This may seem to be drifting into red-braces and 'Brylcreem' territory, but it works! You can walk around while on the call. A smile really does come through on the phone. I once bought myself a headset to do this with, but had to stop when everyone else in the office fell about in stitches.

Close the sale: ask for the business

This is incredibly simple, yet very few businesses do this. You've had a great meeting and are best buddies with your prospect. You leave with warm smiles and get back to your office. But – you don't have anything.

Once you have run through all their possible objections, you must then ask the question: 'So, if we've reassured you on all these points, and met your requirements – can we have the business?' At that stage, they either have to give you another objection (which you answer), or say yes. At the very least, you will know exactly what remaining hurdles are left.

Learn when to shut up

If you are like me, your chosen approach to sales is to jabber excitedly about the product for so long that the customer loses the will to live. That's not a good approach. The object is not to bludgeon them into submission. Listen, nod politely, and let the customer do the selling.

be prepared to keep schtum

As a rule of thumb, you should be talking for less than 50 per cent of a sales meeting.

brilliant tip

Use silence as a negotiation technique

This is something professional buyers are taught. It is very difficult not to rush in and drop your price when your prospect is silent. Be prepared to keep schtum. Repeat a rhyme in your head if it helps (though try not to let your lips move at the same time as this can be a bit disconcerting for others).

Get it in writing

The moment you walk out of your customer's door, your bargaining position is weakening. You have to get them to sign something, anything, there on the spot. Don't expect them to sign a huge contract. Even a simple 'letter of understanding' is good. You can go back with a full contract later.

brilliant tip

If you lose a sale, don't despair. Dial 999.

When you lose a sale or customer, it's sorely tempting to wail and throw your toys out of the pram. Instead, it's time to swallow your pride, and put a plan into action. Call them:

9 days,

9 weeks and

9 months...

after you lost out.

At nine days, they'll possibly be feeling bad for saying no to you. They'll give you some invaluable feedback on why they didn't choose you. Depending on the amount of work you put in, they'll probably give you a referral to someone else who might want your service.

At nine weeks, the fascination with the person they chose instead of you will probably have worn off a bit. Perhaps they should have chosen you after all?

Nine months – well, that's almost a year. Surely it's time they reviewed their decision for the next year?

Should I hire a sales person?

No. OK, not at first.

It's so tempting though. You won't have to do the dirty work. A nice person will come in and do this for you. There are a few reasons to be very cautious about this:

- For a start, it's very hard getting someone good.
- You need to know the job first before you can teach someone else to do it.
- You need to understand your clients – it's the best (though most painful) form of market research.
- If they're any good, they'll be expensive, and in a well-paid position already.
- Using sales agents isn't always ideal as they won't necessarily put the passion into your product that you would.

brilliant recap

This has been a long step, but vital. By now you should:

- Have worked out your sales ratio.
- Come up with a system of rewards/bonuses for yourself.
- Understood what customers are really buying from you.
- Devised a sales script with:
    - open questions
    - answers to common objections
    - a compelling offer.
- Worked out who the decision maker is.
- Learnt how to be a more effective sales person.

STEP 10

Set your price

In this step, we look at why it's important to be as expensive as you can be:

1 How to increase your price.
2 How to feel comfortable with the price you are charging.
3 How to avoid one of the greatest failure hazards: over-trading.

Hold on, I set my price *after* I've sold a product? I've put price here to underline a fundamental point that You Really Must Understand.

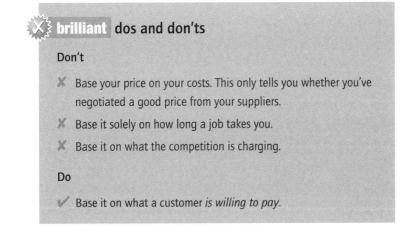

brilliant dos and don'ts

Don't

✘ Base your price on your costs. This only tells you whether you've negotiated a good price from your suppliers.

✘ Base it solely on how long a job takes you.

✘ Base it on what the competition is charging.

Do

✔ Base it on what a customer *is willing to pay*.

This is as much alchemy as science, and can be influenced by a whole host of factors you want to play to your advantage.

What influences price

The factors that influence what a customer is willing to pay include:

- Your perceived expertise. For example:

  Web designer: £40 an hour. Expert in web usability for financial services: £200 an hour.

- The business value of what you are selling. For example:

  Two consultants worked in the oil industry capping wells that gushed. They were happy charging good hourly rates and driving executive cars. Someone pointed out how much they saved an oil company. They swapped their cars for executive helicopters.

- Premium or snob value. For example:

  I'm sitting on a train as I write this. My ticket is £102. The next carriage along is almost identical, but it has little white cloths on the headrests, and free tea. A ticket there costs £350.

- Getting it sooner. For example:

  Hardback Harry Potter: £15. Paperback, six months later: £7.

Be as expensive as you can

brilliant example

I was in a supermarket known for its low approach to prices, looking for some rocket salad (that's how posh I am). It sat in the middle of the row in nice packaging: £1.80.

Then on the bottom row tucked into a corner, I spotted another bag with exactly the same amount. It was unwashed, the packaging was nasty looking: 94p. Of course I grabbed it and skipped cackling joyfully down the aisle.

Even the cheapest supermarkets charge as much as they can possibly get away with for their products. They deliberately sabotage their 'value' brands (I don't mean putting in nails). They put them in cheap and nasty packaging, and hide them in other parts of the store where only value shoppers go. The 'premium' products have little to justify their much higher prices, beyond a string of adjectives. It's not simply 'Bacon', it's 'Finest Maple-cured Canadian Back Bacon'.

The problems with being cheap

Being cheap in business can be extremely difficult to maintain.

brilliant example

In the nineties, an ebullient Frenchman set up a bistro called Pierre Victoire. He wanted to sell cheap French food with a minimum of fuss. He borrowed the food to open up, got the chairs from a charity shop and charged £5 for a set lunch. People loved it. Demand grew.

So he started opening bistros around the UK, and before long he had over 100. But margins were minute: 50 covers at lunch, at £5 a head = £250. Take off the cost of food, staff, overheads. If you smashed a plate at lunchtime, your profit was wiped out. The chain collapsed spectacularly into liquidation, and he left the country.

I'm pleased to say though, he's back now, and like the true entrepreneur is trying it again. Only this time, his prices are that much higher.

You can always come down in price. I don't mean drop your price at the first whiff of trouble. I mean, 'Well, I can offer you a special discount, seeing as it's you,' or, 'I can add an extra service for free.' That way, they feel good, you feel good.

you can always come down in price

Also, once you've dropped your pants on price, it's extremely hard to pull them back up again without looking foolish. The first price you mention in any negotiation is the price around which all subsequent negotiations will be based.

▶ brilliant example

We under-priced a newsletter for a client. We now do jobs for other clients at twice the price, but can only put that one up by 5 per cent without the client feeling they're being ripped off.

People equate price and quality.

▶ brilliant example

I once ran a stall at a university giving away free beer and pakoras to students to promote an Indian restaurant. No-one would come near it. They figured there had to be a catch.

You can't keep it up. If your only competitive edge in business is your low price, you've got problems. There will always be someone cheaper.

▶ brilliant example

The Prince's Trust started up lots of plumbers. Most competed on price. Then all of a sudden there was an influx of Polish plumbers who could do jobs much cheaper. When they get busy, they can bring in their mates from overseas. Until they start to be undercut by the Romanians....

Your customers should squeak at your price

You don't want to win every job you go for. You set your price at £100, you win all 10 clients. Then you have £1,000 and you are knackered. Then you set your price at £200. Three people decline: You make £1,400, and have more time on your hands.

Rent your products

We're familiar with the rental model when it comes to things like cars or DVDs, but with a little creative thinking, there's no end of industries it can be applied to.

brilliant global examples

Californian book store Chegg noticed that students have to fork out large sums for textbooks they only need for a couple of months. So the service allows them to rent the books for a fraction of the sum.

And for kids? German company Lütte Leihen rents out baby clothes through its website. As the nippers grow, customers exchange the products for the next size up.

Levi's in India goes a stage further – rental for jeans. As fashion-conscious but cash-strapped customers often can't afford its premium purchases, its 'pay-as-you-wear' scheme allows them to pay for their new labels in instalments.

Mojo meter: justify your price to yourself

The most common reason people under-price themselves is their lack of self-confidence.

Try the following approaches for size.

Look at what others can charge

brilliant global example

As a young lawyer in South Africa, Joel Joffe campaigned against apartheid. Suddenly he found himself representing Nelson Mandela in court. After the case, Joel realised his time was limited in Africa, so moved to London. Not sure what to do, he co-founded a financial company, Allied Dunbar, which he grew to £250 million. Now he is a Lord, and campaigning on a wide range of issues.

Joel attributes much of his success to a lesson his mother taught him:

Remember, you are no better, but no worse than anyone else.

It's understandable that you don't see yourself as God's gift to business. But look around. Look at your competition. Suddenly you find they are getting away with three times your price! You are certainly as good as them.

look at your competition

Justify the price to yourself

You might think it's greedy to charge too much money when you don't need it. Think instead of what better kit you can invest in or better service you can provide your customers with the higher fee.

Act up to the price

If someone is paying extra, think of how much harder you are going to work to deliver this job for them.

And then, you'll feel great about your price, your customer will feel great about your service, and you'll suddenly realise how rewarding working for yourself can be!

Let your customers trade themselves up

You'd be amazed at how much more certain clients want to pay for a service if you'd only let them. Be inspired by the examples of hardback books and first class travel earlier. Vary your product offering. You can still have your 'standard service' that you know is very price competitive. But then you have a 'deluxe' service, with extra serviettes. Before you know it, customers will be trading themselves up.

> vary your product offering

Increase your price incrementally

I've mentioned how difficult it is to increase prices with existing clients. But there are ways to make your whole customer base more profitable by charging more to new clients beyond a certain capacity. This is the approach airlines use for selling seats.

brilliant example

You run an office cleaning business. You wait until you are at about 65 per cent capacity and then put your prices up by 15 per cent for the next jobs you quote. You don't worry if you lose half of these, because you've already covered your overheads, so this is all 'extra' business.

As that fills up to 80 per cent, do it again but by a bit more. So 20 per cent of your clients are paying 30 per cent more than your original clients, and yet you've still covered your overheads. You'll then gradually want to lose some of your least profitable clients and repeat the process.

Be prepared to lose some customers

Businesses are far too reluctant to do this. You have to be prepared to 'sacrifice the sacred cow'. Low-margin clients can take up a huge amount of your time and effort for very little reward: effort that should be spent on your premium clients.

Push your price up gradually until they walk. You'll often be quite surprised that, despite their huffing and puffing, they're willing to pay extra. Don't fret about them going to the competition. As we've covered elsewhere, competition is a good thing. You are brilliant at your business so don't worry about them.

Avoid 'over-trading'. This is one of the greatest risks to a start-up business and one that ironically hits the most successful businesses. Basically it occurs when you have too much business to handle (imagine!).

Over-trading can happen too easily, and I've seen it occur many times in otherwise great businesses. It goes like this:

> You start with too-low a price. Customers flood in attracted by this. You start to get run ragged, and become knackered, yet you can't afford to hire anyone else to do the work. It's hard to persuade your existing customers to pay more than they are used to.
>
> You are too busy to do invoicing, so your cashflow goes to pot. A machine breaks, and you can't afford to fix it. You hate your business. You go bust.

The price shouldn't come as a shock

Occasionally you'll find a specific job starts growing beyond your expectations. It's tempting to think you should keep schtum and count your good fortune before hitting your client with a whopping bill at the end of the job. But there's a big danger in this. Your client will be horrified. They won't pay, they won't use you again, they'll bad mouth you to others.

brilliant tip

You must keep the customer up to date on price all the way along so there are no nasty surprises.

There is a horrible but compelling analogy of boiling a frog (who makes these up?). If you whack the temperature up to maximum, the frogs will leap out of the water. However, if you gradually edge it up a degree at a time, they don't notice.

I think I need some fresh air.

brilliant recap

Hopefully by now I've convinced you that price is a sales issue, not a financial one.

- You've worked out how to turn your product/service into a premium one.
- You've justified your price to yourself.
- You have a strategy to increase your prices incrementally.
- You've avoided the pitfalls of over-trading.

STEP 11

Now, make your product/ service

It's vital to design your proposition around what customers want. In this step we cover:

1 How to find good suppliers.
2 Creative ways to produce what you want, at a price customers will pay.
3 How to negotiate good prices from suppliers.
4 We also break for a little party!

You sell your product, then you price it, then you make it? Bear with me, there's method in my madness.

I'm trying to emphasise the importance of not designing your proposition in isolation, then pricing it based on what it cost you, then trying to flog it. Although this isn't the way it's taught in business school, it is the way things work in the real world. Your entire proposition must be built solely around satisfying a customer's wants and needs.

So, we know exactly what the customer wants, because they've told us in great detail. We also know what they're prepared to pay for it. Now we have to find a way to deliver this for them, while still making us decent profits.

Find good suppliers

This stage might be a bit harder than you anticipated. As your proposition is uniquely different, you are perhaps doing something no-one has done before. You might be wanting it for cheaper than it has been made before. You probably also want it quicker. Yet you don't have much cash. You don't have credit rating. You don't have purchasing power.

Sounds impossible? Not at all. This is where the brilliant start-ups get going!

How to get the most from your suppliers

This is worth investing considerable effort.

▶ brilliant example

When buying his first plane from Boeing, Richard Branson spent so long in negotiations with them that they threw in the towel. He probably got the cheapest deal they had ever done on a plane. It's not the glamorous stuff he's known for, but it's his ruthless attention to detail that is one of the greatest contributions to his success in business.

It's important not just to squeeze your supplier blatantly for every penny. They've got to win something out of the deal as well. It's more a matter of applying gentle pressure.

Give them the challenge

Suppliers will have far more experience in the sector than you will. So make use of their knowledge. Instead of giving them orders, ask for their advice. Tell them what your budget is, and what your end product will do. Then ask them if they can think of any creative ways to deliver this.

Ask the 'daft laddie/lassie' questions

Don't be afraid to ask the obvious questions.

---

brilliant example

Avril Kennedy was opening a jewellery store. Working with professional surveyors, she noticed they charged a fee based on their hours. 'Hold on', said Avril, 'why don't you just take a percentage of what you save me? That way we both win.' Of course, they'd never done that before, but then no-one had ever asked.

Wince

brilliant tip

Supermarket buyers are trained to wince when a supplier first mentions price. It may be the most fantastic deal they've ever had, but still they wince. You'd be amazed how much further the price will drop when you do.

Look overseas

Distance is only in your imagination. You can often find a much cheaper source of supplies overseas. We live in a small world. It's easier to work with overseas suppliers than you might think and they tend to be amazingly keen.

brilliant example

Clive has an eBay business selling fishing lures. He buys them in bulk from China, repackages them into smaller lots, and then sells them through eBay. He gets orders from all over the world. His suppliers are always sending him new ideas so they can grow together.

Go direct to the manufacturer. You'll often be dealing with an intermediary in the UK. In brilliant business, we don't have time for intermediaries – they get in the way!

Start at the end

You don't have to do it the way it has always been done. The secret is not to start from where you are and try to work forwards. Instead, start with your destination, and think of creative ways to work backwards from there.

brilliant example

I had a business at university publishing yearbooks. I wanted to produce hardback books in runs of 50, for around £5 a book. I went round loads of printers who all fell off their chairs with laughter. The main cost of printing is in the set-up. The cheapest quote I got was £3,000, which worked out at £60 a book.

Then I had a eureka moment. Who said they had to be printed? I found a state-of-the-art photocopier. It could produce photos almost as well as the printer, and was certainly good enough for the students. I got high-quality paper stock and found a binder who could make the pages into hardback. It cost me £2.50 a book to produce.

Build good relationships with your suppliers

Suppliers are one of the most important pieces of your business jigsaw. There is a school of business thought that says: 'Screw your suppliers – don't pay them until taken to court.' I don't agree. You will need them. There will always come a time when you need a favour. You'll need them to do a job for you quickly. You want their insights on what your competitors are up to.

You may not be their largest customer or their best, but if they genuinely like you, then they can do amazing things for you.

Don't get lazy

That said, don't stick with your suppliers year after year solely because of inertia. Make sure that you shop around at least once a year to see if you can get better prices. At the very least, it will keep your **make sure that you shop around** current suppliers on their toes. Think how much harder you'd work if your customers were regularly shopping around?

Manage customers' expectations

brilliant tip

Under-promise – over-deliver.

One of the secrets of success is managing customers' expectations. We've seen how price shouldn't come as a surprise. You also don't want to surprise them by being late with their first order.

Whatever deadline you set yourself – add at least 10 per cent. Jobs always take longer, and if a client is expecting it on a

Wednesday, but you don't deliver until the Friday, they are going to be pretty peeved. Far better to say Friday at the outset, then if you get it to them on the Wednesday they'll be over the moon that you got it to them two days early.

Mojo meter: time for a party!

You've made your first product, you've sold it, you've delivered it early. Your client is delighted. It's time to stop and celebrate!

Business is like a roller-coaster. It's often only a few minutes at the peak of the ride, with happy clients and things going well before you are over the top and on to the next stomach-lurching part of the ride. Which makes it all the more important to celebrate the high points. They move on pretty fast.

brilliant example

I've been known to cartwheel down the office when we win a major new client. Also, when we've produced a publication we were particularly pleased with, we would take it out for a meal. We'd all sit at the table, and have a chair and plate for the magazine to sit at. We'd then toast its health. A number of times.

Wallow in praise. Ask customers how they've found your product or service. Ask them for testimonials. If you get a particularly positive comment then cut it out and stick it over your desk. It'll help when others are grinding you down.

brilliant recap

You've designed your product/service in response to your customers' needs and price. To do this:

- You've found good suppliers.
- You got the most insight you can from them.
- You considered alternative ways to produce your product/service.
- You negotiated a fair price with them.
- You delivered your first order before the customer expected it.
- You found time to celebrate!

STEP 12

Get the
cash in

Poor cashflow is one of the three big failure points for the start-up. In this step we cover an eight-stage cash management system.

Hopefully the hangover from your celebrations has worn off. It's time for a dose of cold water.

There's often a big gap between delivering a product, and getting the cash in the bank.

Watch your cashflow.

A useful set of formulae to remember here is:

- *turnover = vanity*
- *profit = sanity*
- *cash in the bank = reality.*

There is a big difference between having a successful business on paper, and one that actually has the cash in your hot hands. Don't ever under-estimate how bad customers can be at paying.

brilliant example

'We instituted a system of three levels for paying debtors: (1) those from whom solicitors' letters had been received; (2) those from whom a writ had been received; (3) those from whom a writ had been received 14 days ago. My first piece of advice in dealing with creditors is to pay the latter first.'

And who's this nugget from? The former government Minister for Trade and Industry, Lord Heseltine.

Follow this plan for cash management

1 Get payment in advance

It is quite acceptable for suppliers to invoice for a job in stages. Say, a third on commencement, a third at the mid-point and a third at completion. The trick is to stagger the payment times so you get the bulk of the money in before you commit to major purchases yourself.

2 Don't make major purchases on behalf of your customers

You are worried about losing your margin on your purchases. OK, but this shouldn't be your area of greatest margin – you're not adding much value here. And say your mark-up is 10 per cent. Fine, but if you run out of cash, you'll be borrowing at up to 20 per cent, so it's little comfort.

clients will appreciate your openness

Clients will appreciate your openness. You can also charge them 'handling fees' for managing purchasing on their behalf, picking items up, negotiating, etc. – and this can often cover your lost mark-up. It also protects you from mishap.

example

A new start agency was producing a large magazine for a high-street chain. The print bill was around £100,000. It took delivery of the lovely magazine, and admired it, until someone spotted the biggest word on the cover 'summmer' (sic). Oh. My. God. After a lot of shoving, the MD called the client with the horror news. Before he could get into the conversation, the client responded 'and we love how you put an extra 'm' in 'summer' – mmm!'

3 Don't give credit

It's an assumption that you always have to give customers credit terms. Who says? It's the equivalent to lending them money. OK, so they might stipulate it as the price of doing business, but even then, I'd negotiate the terms. Once you've been working with a customer for a while, and they've paid you promptly, then you might consider it.

4 Negotiate good supplier terms

I know it's obvious, but people don't realise these are negotiable. Perhaps you can stage pay your supplier, or pay a slight premium if you can pay 60 days later. I recently interviewed an entrepreneur who took over an engineering business without spending a penny, just by manipulating his customer and supplier payment terms.

5 Consider factoring

Otherwise known as 'invoice discounting', this is where a bank or specialist factoring firm takes over your invoice collection. It pays you a sum immediately, then the balance when it receives payment. For this, it makes a small percentage charge against the invoice.

OK, so there's a cost against this, but weigh it against the future growth of your business.

6 Develop a rigorous system

Issue an invoice the moment a job is complete. If possible, phone the customer in advance to let them know what this sum is going to be – that stops them disputing it a month later.

The day it falls due, phone them, and ask when you can expect payment. Chances are they'll give you the immortal kiss-off line 'the cheque's in the post'. Fine, but take them at their word: 'Great, so I can expect payment arriving in two days maximum?' Then call them again on that morning to request payment.

If nothing arrives, then send the customer a 'legal letter'. This is a simple template that threatens legal action in five days if they don't pay. You might want to follow this up with a letter announcing your lawyers are commencing action. All the time, be as polite and courteous as you can. But firm.

This all sounds a little drastic? It shouldn't. So far the cost to you is a few quick calls and 90p in stamps. And many companies will have a policy of not paying until this stage anyway.

7 Become an irritant

OK, it's got serious. They are still not paying. What next? This is time to copy the approach of the late 'Payment Chicken'. This was a great French business idea whereby you could pay for a large yellow chicken to follow your debtors around until they coughed up. You don't have to go that far. But turning up in the client's reception, and generally hanging around like a bad smell is a great way to get payment.

> hanging around like a bad smell is a great way to get payment

8 Consider legal action

See how I've left this until last? It should be your last resort too. This process can be very time consuming and costly. And even if you win, there's no guarantee you'll receive payment even then.

brilliant recap

You now have a cash management system, including:

- Advance payments.
- No automatic credit.
- Good supplier terms.
- A regular system.
- A 'legal letter' template.

STEP 13

Do your books

Watching your finances is essential. In this step, we:

1 Devise a simple book-keeping system.

2 Look at the merits of hiring a book-keeper.

3 Cover the pitfalls of dealing in cash.

4 Run through the main tax issues.

5 See how to avoid tax legally.

We've skated fairly lightly over paperwork so far. This is because 'good systems' won't make you a success. However, having none at all can quickly flatten an otherwise successful business.

Don't worry, I'll make this as painless as possible…

Keep your book-keeping system simple

Simple, but disciplined.

Many small businesses operate the 'box under the bed' system of book-keeping. They then turn up at an accountant two days before a tax deadline with handfuls of paper and ask them to complete their return. There are obvious downsides to this approach:

- You'll rack up large accountancy fees.
- You'll probably come to the attention of the Revenue, who'll want to inspect you (and then want to go all the way back over any previous years' figures).
- There's the risk of late payment fines and interest payments.

But there is a more important risk:

- You won't know on a day-to-day basis if you are making money.

It's like setting off to sea without a map or compass (or whatever they use these days). To keep the basic systems, do the following.

Keep a record of everything you purchase, and a record of everything you sell

File all your receipts and invoices in date order. When you purchase things, ask for a VAT receipt and not just a credit card receipt (this particularly applies to petrol stations and restaurants). If you don't get a receipt, then it's hard to claim tax back against your tax bill.

Put a number on the top of each receipt. When you receive payment, put a note on the invoice and the date of payment.

Your invoices don't have to be at all fancy (though see Step 16 on branding). You just need the date, your name and address, your invoice number, the customer name and the amount. If you are a limited company, you also need to include your company number. If you are registered for VAT, you will also need to include the amount of VAT and your VAT number.

> your invoices don't have to be at all fancy

Enter these records into your 'books'

This can literally be a set of books. Manual accounting systems are perfectly acceptable and work fine. Enter all your expenses into a 'purchase ledger', and your sales into your 'sales ledger'. Alternatively, buy a simple piece of book-keeping software. There are many great ones on the market. I'd avoid anything overly complex at this stage. It's easy to upgrade your systems as you grow.

From this, you'll get a position of your profit and loss on a month-by-month basis. But that's not it.

'Reconcile' your accounts

This is the bit that can turn you prematurely grey. You'll often find that what your books tell you should be in your bank account, and what's actually there, are a very different matter. And your bank balance doesn't lie. Therefore, you have to go through your bank statements and tick off every item against your books. Then go through your books and find any payments not listed (i.e. those you made with petty cash). Where the figures don't tally (i.e. you have a missing receipt), then make an entry showing this in your books.

At the end of the exercise your sets of figures should match up. Should.

Make sure you hold on to these records at the end of the year. The Revenue requires you to keep tax records for five years, and six years for VAT.

Hire a book-keeper

Some people love book-keeping. It gives them a deep sense of peace that all is right in the world. I salute them. Personally

I'd rather eat warm gravel than do my books. But that doesn't mean you can avoid them. So fairly early on in my business, I made a 'star-signing'. I employed 'Aunty Nan'. Nan has been a book-keeper for many years (I won't say how many), and gets very upset if our figures don't tally – even by pennies. And woe-betide anyone who's claiming for a newspaper without a receipt. Our figures are always spot on. And I sleep very peacefully at night.

So, you need to have a very good knowledge of how much money you have in the bank all the time. You need to know where you are making profit, or not. The cost of a part-time book-keeper should be minimal and you probably only need them for a few hours a week. (I wouldn't use your accountant for this, unless they are particularly cheap or you have very simple records.) And don't forget the opportunity cost of your time – all that time gnawing a pencil you could be out selling!

Be careful with cash

Entrepreneurs love cash. Mmmm! Lovely crisp notes! However, cash can present problems for your business systems.

For many of your smaller purchases, you'll be using cash from your own pocket. That's fine, just make sure you get receipts for all of these. Then enter them into your books at the end of the month, and pay yourself a cheque from the business. Don't get into the habit of mixing up your personal and business bank accounts. It can also help to get either a business credit card or a personal one that you use only for your business.

entrepreneurs love cash

When you get paid in cash, then you've got a different problem:

You've delivered a service or product that morning. Your customer is canny, and negotiates a 'discount for cash'. They peel off a wad of grubby bank notes for you. Then you find yourself in the pub that evening, with a wallet full of cash and a thirst. You think, 'Well, if I declare this cash through my business, I'll have to pay tax on it, and I've already given a discount...'

The only thing I'll say here is that putting cash in your back pocket and not declaring it, while very tempting, can lead to much bigger problems. For a start, it's sloppy thinking, and you'll never get an accurate picture of your business. And, surprisingly, you are not the first person to have thought of this.

The Revenue are very alive to the industry sectors and types of businesses that operate cash in hand. It'll want very accurate records for all your cash. It'll compare you with what businesses like you should be declaring. Tax inspectors have been known to snoop through small ads and then check the businesses listed have declared the income in their returns. This is a world of pain you just don't want to enter.

To my mind, the whole point of being self-employed is to live a life free from worry, obligation and control. If you have to spend your whole life looking over your shoulder for the taxman or being shopped by a disgruntled customer/employee, then it ain't worth it.

Tax

Yep, it's that time. I'm not going to give an exhaustive guide to tax bands and rates. The best place for this is HMRC itself with its simple start-up section: **www.hmrc.gov.uk/startingup/index.htm**.

The following are the types of tax you will be expected to pay (not including your personal income tax).

Corporation tax

If you are a limited company, this is the tax on the profits you make at the year end. Remember, if you are not a limited company, you only pay personal income tax, but pay it on all your profits (see Step 8).

National Insurance (NI)

As well as your personal National Insurance, you'll have to pay NI on top of the cost of employing someone. We come on to employment later (in Step 15), and this isn't a reason to put off employing someone, but a word of caution.

Employed or self-employed?

If someone does work for you, but is not an employee, then you don't have to pay NI. However, this means it's tempting to pretend part-time staff members are not actually employed by you to dodge the NI.

Of course, HMRC are canny to this. They will check the person's status, whether they work a consistent number of days for you, how much work they do for other people, whether you pay them a consistent lump sum. If they decide the person is actually an employee they can hit you for all the back NI you should have paid.

VAT

If you expect your total turnover (all the money you receive, not profits) to exceed £73,000 (for 2011–12) in the first year, then you must register for Value-Added Tax. VAT is an insidious charge that gets added to every stage of a transaction as it passes through people's hands. You can claim it back on things you buy, but you have to charge it on most things you sell.

you can claim it back on things you buy

The main band of VAT is 20 per cent, and if you are over the £73,000 threshold (for 2011–12), then you need to add VAT to the cost of your product/service. There are certain products that are exempt or zero-rated for VAT. This can be a very complex area (HMRC lost a long-running VAT battle as to whether Marks & Spencer teacakes are 'cakes' or 'biscuits'), so seek advice if you think your business might fall into this area. *VAT Notice 700* on the HMRC website gives a guide to this area but basically examples of exempt or zero-rated products are:

- food (but not 'hot prepared food' or confectionery)
- books and publications (depending on level of advertising, amount of words, etc.)
- children's clothing
- exports
- training and education services.

The VAT system

Accounting and claiming for VAT is one of the most irritating bits of being in business. Essentially you are acting as a tax collector for the Revenue. The Revenue has therefore looked to simplify the system by setting up the Flat Rate Scheme for small businesses.

If your business turns over less than £187,500, you can apply to join the scheme. Then you simply calculate a fixed percentage of your turnover in a given period, and send it to the Revenue. The fixed percentage varies from profession to profession so check carefully what you will be expected to pay. Because it's an average, you can't be on the Flat Rate Scheme and still claim back VAT on purchases except in a few cases.

There is also an Annual Accounting Scheme. Below a set turn-over level, you can work out with the Revenue an estimated amount for the year, based on your previous year's return. You then pay this monthly by direct debit, with a balancing adjustment at the end of the year. You can adjust this throughout the year if circumstances change.

To help your cashflow, there is a further scheme called Cash Accounting. Here you only pay tax when you receive payment, not when you issue an invoice.

If any of these schemes interest you, go to the Revenue website and read up on it, or call the helpline on 0845 010 9000. VAT is a complex area so do seek advice.

How to pay less tax

The easiest way is to ensure you have very detailed records, and have claimed everything back that you can.

Tax credits

There are also tax credits you might be due: see **www.hmrc.gov. uk/startingup/payless.htm**.

Working tax credit

If you are self-employed and surviving off a low income as your business gets off the ground, then there are credits available for you.

Child tax credit and disability

Again, check the website to see if you qualify.

Research

You can also claim back tax credits for research and development you undertake in your business: see **www.hmrc.gov.uk/ randd/index.htm**.

Buying equipment

The shock for most start-ups is that you can't claim back the total cost of a new piece of equipment in the year in which you bought it. Instead, you have to claim back a 'capital allowance' each year reflecting your length of ownership of a piece of equipment (around 40 per cent, less for cars and subject to change: see **www.hmrc.gov.uk/capital_allowances/investmentschemes.htm**).

You used to be able to claim back 100 per cent of computer and related equipment in the first year, but this is no longer the case.

Claim back everything you are allowed to

While you want to claim for as much as possible, the rules around this are fairly tight, so be warned. The following is a guide, but I'm not a tax expert, and regulations change quickly so take professional advice.

take professional advice

- Working from home. You used to be able to claim a proportion of your rent/mortgage. However, the guidance is now 'additional costs you incur'. Therefore, unless you build a new room for the purpose of your business it might be tricky. You can however claim back the additional heating, lighting and phone bills you incur. If you build an office in your garden shed (I've known many who have!) then beware of business rates.

- Travelling. You can claim travel that is solely for business. You can also claim 'subsistence' – the food and drink you consume on these trips (but there are limits). You cannot claim the cost of travelling to and from your place of work, nor parking/motor fines.

- Fuel costs are tricky. It is probably simpler to keep your car, fuel and running costs out of the business, but claim back an amount per mile (around 45p) for business mileage you do. Keep a record of all your work journeys and petrol receipts.

- Entertaining. You cannot claim back the cost of entertaining clients, but you can claim the cost of business gifts (up to a limit). You can claim back the cost of entertaining staff, but again up to a limit.

Of course, there are grey areas here the astute can take advantage of (a friend put her state of the art hi-fi system through the business as 'staff training equipment') but be very careful. Even if while you are on a business trip, you take a day's holiday, the Revenue will want to deduct for this.

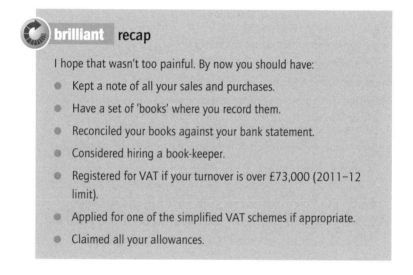

brilliant recap

I hope that wasn't too painful. By now you should have:

- Kept a note of all your sales and purchases.
- Have a set of 'books' where you record them.
- Reconciled your books against your bank statement.
- Considered hiring a book-keeper.
- Registered for VAT if your turnover is over £73,000 (2011–12 limit).
- Applied for one of the simplified VAT schemes if appropriate.
- Claimed all your allowances.

STEP 14

Do a quick risk audit

You are now up and running, the business is going well, and you are over the 'start-up hump'. You are not out of the woods yet – it's time to do a quick 'risk check' on your business.

Risk check

We've been mentioning risks as we have gone along, mainly under **'Hazards!'**, but let's just check you've got them covered.

Have you protected your ideas?

- You should have registered your designs.
- Posted any copyright material to yourself.
- Considered a trade mark for your identity.
- Completed non-disclosure agreements with suppliers, staff and contacts.

Done a legal MOT with your lawyers

To cover:

- client contracts
- supplier terms and conditions
- employment contracts.

Under finance

- Got rid of any personal guarantees on your borrowing, or be within close distance of this.
- Have at least 80 per cent of your clients paying within 60 days.
- Know exactly how much money you have in the bank, and this ideally to be equal to one month's turnover.

Under insurance

- Have adequate insurance for your main business assets.

Under sales

- Be spending the majority of your time selling.
- Have either a 'sales funnel' full of at least 14 leads, or a minimum 5 per cent increase in new sales every month.
- Have a price high enough that you lose a small proportion of your customers.

Under 'you'

- Be enjoying yourself.

Mojo meter: coping when things go wrong

By now you will have had your fair share of scrapes and bumps. It's important you realise you are not uniquely rubbish at business. If you get slightly more right than you get wrong, I think you are doing pretty well.

Understandably, people are nervous about talking about their business failures. But read about great inventors and entrepreneurs through history, like Eddison and the light-bulb, and you realise how many failures they went through. It's an inevitable part of the

fail quickly, cheaply and don't take it personally!

creative process. The secret is to fail quickly, cheaply and don't take it personally!

One of the best bits of advice I got from a mentor was: 'Learn crying as a negotiation technique.' It sounds a bit harsh at first, but it's true. If you make a mistake, don't try to hide from it.

---

brilliant example

When I started off publishing yearbooks, I used to do all the typing myself. Finishing a book late one night, I didn't notice the spell checker had 'corrected' the name of the class president, Angus MacDonald, by taking the 'g' out of his first name. I shipped the books off to be printed in China and it wasn't until the graduation day that someone spotted the mistake.

I was mortified. I grovelled in humble apology. I offered to reprint the books. I offered to apologise personally to Angus. However, the students just thought it was funny and I got away with it.

What you'll often find is that customers become more loyal to you after you've made a mistake. Everyone accepts life doesn't always go to plan. An early and upfront admission of a problem, and how you are going to fix it, will often reassure a customer. There is also little as disarming in life as a heart-felt apology, and it will usually defuse any tricky situation.

PHASE 3

Up and running

Congratulations! You have a fully functioning business. You should feel justly proud of your efforts.

In this phase, we're going to look at keeping your business running smoothly without going demented yourself.

Step 15 Taking on staff

Step 16 Make sales easier: marketing

STEP 15

Taking on staff

Your business is growing so it's now time to evaluate whether you should take on staff. We look at:

1 Which bits of your job you should stop doing.
2 Cheap ways to outsource work.
3 Where to find good employees.
4 How to interview.
5 Legal issues for employees.

How to know when it's time to employ staff

You have to work out your own cost to your business by following these three steps.

1 Work out where you are 'adding value'

Write out a timesheet, and fill it out for one week. At the end of the week, go through the list of things you've done, and rank where you add the most value. This is the area that will advance your business the furthest in the long term, and couldn't be done by anyone else.

Then work out what percentage of your time you spend doing this really productive stuff, and how much of your time is just spent doing work others could do.

2 Work out your 'opportunity cost'

The trouble too many owners fall into is that they treat everything in the business as a cost, except for their own time. The cost of your time in the business is not what you are saving by doing work yourself, it is the long-term value you could be building. You want to grow your business to £150,000 in your first year? Your opportunity cost therefore is roughly £90 an hour.

3 Outsource everything you can

If it costs less than your hourly rate to get someone to do a job for you, then you should get them to do it. This frees your time up to grow your business. So, outsource as many of the non-essential jobs from your timesheet as you can, for example, book-keeping, couriers, manufacturing. This should leave you free to concentrate on the tasks that really grow your business long-term, such as sales.

this frees your time up to grow your business

brilliant example

I was listening to someone who wanted to set up an Italian bakery. 'Where will you get your supplies?' I asked. 'I'll drive to Italy to pick them up because that'll be cheaper,' came the answer.

Having picked myself up off the floor, I pointed out the maths. That's three days of driving. He'll save perhaps £125 in courier costs. I can't believe he couldn't generate 10 times that if he spent the time going out and visiting customers, finding other suppliers, checking the competition and looking for savings.

And for those jobs you can't oursource, you'll need to take on staff.

Mojo meter: take time off

Have you had the following conversation with a fellow small business owner recently?

You   I'm knackered, I had to get up at 6 this morning...

Friend   That's nothing, I got up at 6, but only went to bed at 2am.

You   Lucky sod! I may have got up at 6, but now I'm going to work a 28-hour day, and my next day off is in three weeks.

There's no doubt it took you long hours to get your business to this stage. But that doesn't mean you have to become a complete masochist about things. Nobody can work at full capacity for long periods (in fact, the maximum length for full concentration is only 40 minutes). You'll find your decision making gets worse, as does your creativity and passion. It'll start to rub off on your customers.

More often, you're chaining yourself to work out of a sense of guilt. And work has a nasty habit of expanding to fit the time available. So, it's essential to give yourself a break. The whole point of working for yourself is being able to control your hours. If you make a good sale or call – give yourself the rest of the day off. Go and see a matinee at the cinema, go for a long walk in the country. You'll come back refreshed, energised and far more effective.

'Throw a sicky.' You know the days when things just don't look so great. If you force yourself into work you'll only pro-long your illness. And don't scrimp on holidays. It's a shock, but you'll often find you are not as irreplaceable as you thought you were. Which brings us nicely on to staff and delegation…

brilliant tip

Don't become irreplaceable. Many people console themselves that they're the only one who can do a job perfectly. While flattering to the ego, that's not a good place to be. You'll never grow the business and might have just bought yourself an expensive job.

Where to find good employees

Recruitment can be an expensive process, so it's best to start off using your own channels first.

Free options

Ask around your own network. This can be larger than you think. Ask friends and family, but don't automatically employ them. It might seem an easy answer in the short term, but become an emotional minefield longer term.

Ask suppliers. They'll possibly be dealing with your competitors, and know a disgruntled staff member. Ask customers. Again they might know your industry. Put an advert on your website, or try web forums and newsgroups in your industry. Ask the local enterprise agency and/or council.

Social media is also a help here. Put a note on your LinkedIn profile, Facebook or Twitter.

You might also want to incentivise people to find staff. Large companies pay thousands for staff referrals, but in a small business a nice bottle of wine can be a sufficient token of appreciation.

The government can help you. The most obvious place to look is Job Centres, but local enterprise organisations often have programmes such as 'women returners' or schemes for placing enthusiastic graduates with local companies. Also consider local university, college and school career offices.

the government can help you

Commercial options

If the above don't work, consider advertising. Look at online job boards. Also consider smaller line adverts in the recruitment sections – these can work as well as larger display adverts at a fraction of the cost.

For highly skilled jobs, don't rule out recruitment agencies. Sure, they'll charge you a percentage of the person's first year salary, but you can negotiate hard on this. They'll save you the cost of advertising, and hopefully have a good stock of very suitable candidates.

How to interview for staff

This is not an area on which to cut corners.

Draw up a detailed job description

A sample is shown overleaf.

Ensure that as well as the tasks they'll do and *skills* they'll need, make sure you also include the *attitudes*. These can often be more important.

Job description	Shop assistant			
Person interviewed	Jennifer Hopeful			
Attitudes needed	Friendly and likes working with people			
	Reliable – will turn up on time			
	Previous shop experience			
	Enthusiastic – will muck in			
Skills needed	Ability to work with customers			
	Basic maths			
Notes				
Score out of 10	Friendliness	Enthusiasm	Reliability	Experience

brilliant example

You are running a café. The most important skill I would imagine for a waitress is a pleasant and outgoing personality. So what if they don't have experience or food handling qualifications? You can teach those. But you can't teach the right attitude.

Beware of hiring a clone of yourself. Sure, your new production manager is a hoot. They laugh at the same jokes as you, and love to go around chatting to clients. But what happens if they share the same lax attitude and scant attention to detail as you? If you've done a good analysis of your skills and weaknesses (Step 1), you won't actually have much in common with your new employee. But the pair of you may just be the perfect fit.

Also, be wary of the softer skills staff need in a small business. They need to be self-motivated, trustworthy and able to work on their own. Someone coming from the relative security (ha!) of a large company might freak out at what's required in a small business.

Treat the interview as a sales exercise – for you!

The onus is on you to find out if this person is right for your business. So beforehand, write down the types of questions that will help you find out. You need open-ended questions such as, 'What type of work environment do you like?', 'What aspects of your last job did you most and least enjoy?', 'What type of job would you like to be doing in 5/10 years?' Don't ask 'Are you reliable?' and expect a heartfelt confession.

In the interview, make the prospect feel relaxed, so they're more natural. Also, start off with a good sales job on your business to them. You don't want to find a dream recruit turns you down.

> you don't want to find a dream recruit turns you down

Check up on them

As a sales person, you'll know there's often a bit of a gap between what people say and what they can actually do. Again, it's up to you to dig:

- You can give them an exercise or practical test to complete (this can be a real eye-opener).
- Ask them to bring evidence to the interview. This could be a portfolio, or for a sales person their previous pay slips.
- If it's essential to get an honest answer to a question, try asking the same question in three different ways.
- Tell them you'll be taking up references. That way they'll be more inclined to be truthful.

And make sure you do follow up references. It's laziness not to, and previous employers have a degree of legal obligation to tell you the truth. If interviewees can't provide a reference for recent jobs, then perhaps that will ring alarm bells (unless of course they haven't told their current employer they might be leaving). You can also ask other people who might have dealt with them, like clients and suppliers.

Be objective

Immediately after the interview, sit down, and rate them on your scorecard. Of course, listen to your gut feeling about the person, but make sure you are not being swayed by one aspect of their personality that is not really relevant to the job.

Employment legal issues

How I wish I could cover this in one paragraph! Sadly, there are more regulations around employing people than there are in almost any other aspect of business. These can cover age, ethnicity, disability, gender, nationality, religious beliefs, minimum wage, and health and safety.

What I can do is point you towards a simple interactive tool the government has produced. It allows you to check the specifics of your job, and the person you are looking to recruit for it. Go to **www.businesslink.gov.uk** and look under 'Employment and Skills – recruiting people – finding new people'. The tool is called 'check your legal responsibilities'.

I would also recommend getting legal support around employment issues. I wouldn't necessarily go straight to a lawyer however, as the costs could rack up for some fairly generic advice. Instead, try a helpline service such as the Federation of Small Businesses (FSB) which is free as part of its annual fee. Other small business services provide similar advice.

Mojo meter: sacking someone

This has to be one of the worst things you have to do in business. Perhaps the person is not working out in the way you'd hoped. Perhaps there isn't enough work to keep them. But, you cannot put off making tough decisions in business. Delaying won't make them easier for either of you, and may make the problem worse. Having thoroughly checked the legal position, you just have to grasp the nettle.

brilliant example

I once had to sack a good friend. I'd fretted about it for about four months. It wasn't working out and the atmosphere was becoming increasingly tense. I finally plucked up the courage to broach the subject. We had a frank discussion, and parted company, while keeping our respect and friendship intact. The moment we'd talked, I felt my shoulders lifting from months of stress.

brilliant recap

As you grow, taking on staff might be an option, but to decide this you should have:

- Completed a time sheet to see where you add the most value.
- Calculated your hourly cost to the business.
- Outsourced non-core activities.
- Used cheap recruitment methods.
- Drawn up a realistic job description.
- Interviewed professionally.
- Conducted a quick online legal audit on your proposed employee.
- Joined the FSB or similar advice service.

STEP 16

Make sales easier: marketing

In this step we cover:

1 Branding.

2 Why to start with your existing customers.

3 How to build 'word of mouth'.

4 The different marketing approaches:

- direct marketing

- digital and online marketing

- social media

- public relations

- advertising.

You might be surprised to find this step towards the end of the book. We've covered product, price and place – which are all part of marketing. What we're looking specifically at here is 'promotion'. I've stuck it at the end so you avoid the pitfall of many start-ups: 'I don't have to do the horrible job of selling because I can just do some nice glossy marketing instead.' Well, I'm sorry, but I believe marketing should principally exist to make your sales job a bit easier. It can never be a replacement for the hard bit of going out and hustling – however much you might hate doing it. You're also not going to produce good marketing until you really understand your sales process.

Branding

This is a big word for a very small idea: reassurance.

Going back to psychology, it's down to something called 'Fear of Regret'. When we are looking to buy something, there is a large amount of worry. Could I have bought it cheaper, will they let me down, will it break, will there be a better one coming out soon? That's why big companies spend millions on their marketing – to reassure customers that they've made the right choice.

reassure customers that they've made the right choice

brilliant example

They used to say 'no-one ever got sacked for buying an IBM computer'. The company spent millions at its colour research unit devising the 'IBM Big Blue' colour which they felt provided a sense of loyalty, depth and love.

Happily for us, there are cheaper ways to do this.

Use smoke and mirrors

brilliant example

An entrepreneur was starting a document storage business, but he had few clients. When prospects visited his warehouse, they saw row after row of empty shelves. So, taking the 'Wizard of Oz' approach literally, he lined the walls of the warehouse with mirrors behind the existing boxes. Hey presto – prospects walked in, saw the place was packed, and gave him the order.

There are simple ways to do this. If you are a sole trader, always talk about 'we' rather than 'I'. Get good testimonials from big clients. Sure, you may have only delivered computers for them, but that doesn't stop you from putting 'Sony' on your client list.

brilliant example

I used to drive an old Renault 5 my colleagues charitably called 'Bozo the Clown's Car'. Not only did it look a little bashed but neither the driver's door nor window opened. Having been to a particular client meeting, my colleague and I were horrified to be followed by the client into the car park. We walked nonchalantly past my car, went round the corner, and hid in a bush until he'd gone back inside. We then drove carefully out of the car park keeping our heads below the dashboard.

Consistency

...creates reassurance. The more consistently you apply your brand and make the customer experience, the more reassured they will be. It's not about spending lots of money. If you have a shop, then make sure the brand is on the front window, the carpet, the uniforms the staff are wearing, the price tags, the mirror in the changing room and on the carrier bag customers take away. This implies you are professional and established. Pret A Manger go so far as putting their logo in chocolate sprinkles on their cappuccinos. Sweet.

Put yourself in the shop window

You have one huge advantage over your big competitors – *your butt is on the line*. I'm serious. If you know that a supplier is not going to eat supper that night unless they give you a good service, then you are going to be pretty reassured about their commitment.

So don't hide behind a large faceless brand. Let them know it is you who are the driving force in the business. Give them your direct phone number. Give them your personal guarantee.

Keep your customers and sell them more stuff: cross and up-selling

Don't run around like a headless chicken trying to sell to everyone. Start with the customers you've got. Use the following three steps.

1 Hold on to your existing customers

Before you even think about getting new clients, you must ensure you keep your existing ones happy. It sounds obvious, but you'd be amazed how many huge companies overlook this.

As I'm writing this, we are in the midst of a downturn, and large companies are suddenly waking up to the value of their existing customers rather than just new ones. As one of the wealthiest men in the world, Warren Buffett said: 'It's only when the tide goes out do you discover who's been swimming naked.'

Loyal customers have a number of advantages:

- they will often pay higher prices because they trust you (and you know how much you can get away with charging them!)
- it is easier to sell them additional things
- they cost less to service – you know what they need, and they know what you supply.

You don't have to get too fancy about this. As (stereotypically) a French loyalty expert said: 'You cannot keep your lover faithful by awarding them points, and then offering to double them if they stay until breakfast.' So perhaps not surprisingly, the most frequent business flyers are 'loyal' to an average of four different airline loyalty schemes.

It's far simpler than that. Just keep in contact with customers. Give them a call or visit on a regular basis. If you've more than a few, then do a mailing to them – a letter or newsletter. Remember, it helps if you 'bait the hook'. Give them something of value in this – inform, educate and entertain them. No-one likes a person who talks about themselves all the time.

> **it helps if you 'bait the hook'**

2 Cross-sell

Once you've got a good customer, try to sell them lots more stuff.

> ### brilliant tip
>
> It is five times easier to sell to an existing client than it is to a new one.

It has taken a customer a lot of trust to purchase something from you, and that trust is worth a lot. Make the most of it. Think of other products you can flog them. It can be as simple as the, 'Do you want fries with that?' question.

If you've sold them a sandwich at lunchtime, would they like a 'supper pack', or catering for a function? You've cleaned their windows, so what about a glass replacement service? Think laterally – OK, you might not have the service yourself, but you can refer someone else to do the work and take a commission. It is far, far easier to do this than continually having to win over new clients.

3 Get people talking about your business

Personal recommendations count for a lot. If you can get people talking about your business, and your marketing, not only is it free advertising, but it's much more believable and trustworthy.

▶ brilliant global example

Every year, on 1 April, BMW reveals a new 'innovation' for its cars. 2008's was the Canine Repellent Alloy Protection (you can figure it out) showing a slightly smouldering dog standing next to a car it had just relieved itself against. See **www.bmweducation.co.uk/coFacts/linkDocs/ caninerepellent.asp**.

People forwarded the link to their friends round the world, and BMW got millions of pounds' worth of free advertising.

If you are lucky, this can happen all on its own, but there are some ways to give it a helping hand.

brilliant tips

1   Make your marketing distinctive and catchy. Look at the steps we identified in super-charging your idea (Step 2).

2   Ask all your customers if there's anyone they would recommend you to. Chase up the leads yourself rather than waiting for them to do it.

3   Reward them. It can be as little as saying thank you for their referral, and letting them know how important it is for your business. You could send them a bottle of wine as thanks. You can offer them a small discount on their next order.

4   Make it easy. Make sure customers have your phone number to hand. Little things like pens, mouse-mats, carrier bags can all make this so much easier.

Different marketing approaches

Only once you have held on to your existing customers, cross-sold them everything you can think of, and mined their referrals should you then start looking at other forms of promotion.

Direct marketing

You may think of it as the awful letters from personal loan companies that clutter your doormat. There is an element of truth to this. If your promotion is poorly thought out, then you can do more harm than good. I knew of a window cleaning business that put a series of leaflets on car windows, designed in the style of parking tickets. They were mystified that potential customers didn't beat a path to their door.

However, if you follow some sensible steps, direct marketing can be a cost-effective source of leads.

brilliant tips

1 Make sure you've got a good address list. If possible, do a quick call first to check the contact details are right. (While you are at it, why not ask if they are the right person to send information to – you will already be two steps along your sales funnel.) Don't just bump up your numbers with poor quality leads. Also, check you are not mailing to people who have registered with the Mailing Preference Service not to receive direct mail (**www.mpsonline.org.uk**).

2 Make your offer compelling. There has to be a real value to customers in what you are offering. Put the clear benefit in the headline. Tailor it to your audience (not 'window cleaning' but 'specialised Edinburgh window cleaning for high-rise buildings').

▶

3   Make it different: it's a theme I can't stress enough. You don't have the budget to compete with big brands, so you have to out-think them with an original marketing idea.
4   Get someone else to proofread your letter and check your data.
5   Follow up your mailing with a call. It can increase your response rate five-fold.

▶ brilliant examples

Of how not to do it

A big UK company ran a campaign targeting small businesses on the theme of 'bring your business back to us'. They sent out boxes with live carrier pigeons inside. Only they missed the delivery slot, and all the boxes arrived on Saturday morning to companies that were closed for the weekend...

A wealth management company ran a campaign targeting wealthy investors. A temp had been brought in to do the mailmerge but no-one did a proofing test of the campaign before sending the letters off. The envelopes were fine, it's just that they all contained a letter which started 'Dear capitalist bastard...'

Online marketing

We've covered e-commerce earlier (see Step 6). Now we consider the internet as a marketing channel. Very few businesses exist these days without a website. But before rushing into it, it's worth just asking yourself the following question: Are your customers strangers?

If the majority of your customers are strangers…

…then your website can be a valuable tool to reach new customers. Design your site to hook skim readers. This can mean having more text on your home page so it's picked up by search engines. Also, the front-end of your site might have to be quite broad and 'shallow'.

Getting people to your site can take considerable investment. This can take the form of:

- regular search engine optimisation (SEO)
- bidding for Google ad words
- promoting yourself through relevant forums
- paying for banner adverts on other sites.

A note on SEO: I'm not going into the intricacies of SEO techniques here, as whatever I say will be out of date pretty much before this book hits the shelves. All I would say is to follow the lessons relating to any form of marketing.

Firstly, work out your return on investment. When factoring in the cost, make sure you include your own time. It's easy to be seduced by the fact that much social media is free. However, once you factor in the time it takes you to produce and update the content, and multiply that by your hourly rate, it puts the results into sharp relief.

Then be brutally honest about those results. You may be getting a satisfying number of hits on your site, or click-throughs from an e-mail newsletter. But how many actually go on to purchase from you? Would you have got better results from taking all that time and directly phoning or meeting potential customers?

> be brutally honest about those results

If you know the majority of your customers already…
…it's likely your website will mainly be useful for reassurance. In this case you can afford to have more graphics on your front page as you want to make more of a brand statement and are less concerned about coming out top on a random search.

Your site can also be 'deeper' with more content. You don't have to worry about fickle readers clicking away. Customers might want to know more about the people behind your business, so a blog might be an option.

Finally, you will want to build in tools to get people to return, particularly e-mail newsletters.

Social media

As a way to reach new customers, you'd be mad to ignore social media. But as with most new technologies, it's worth applying the 'shiny kit' test: is it genuinely useful, or is it just something glittering and cool, but ultimately pointless?

The best way to do this is to start with what you actually want to use social media for.

Gaining publicity

Social media sites like Twitter, Facebook, YouTube and LinkedIn can be an excellent free way to build publicity for your business, and for your potential customers to get to know more about you. The transparency of many such sites is also an excellent way of building trust, particularly if you can get satisfied customers to rate your service positively.

For great results, why not make the most of the temporary nature of the internet to build a sense of excitement and exclusivity around your brand. Rather than the 'always available' nature of retail, a number of stores have short-notice sales, with limited amounts of stock and a short deadline.

> make the most of the temporary nature of the internet

brilliant global example

Russian online store KupiVIP gets members to sign-up to its store and then drives their behaviour with short-notice and limited offer sales. The sense of scarcity encourages customers to make instant decisions, and part with the cash quickly!

Improving customer service

For the more adventurous, social media can transform the way you go about business in a whole raft of ways.

brilliant global examples

For Korean food outlet Kogi BBQ, Twitter is at the core of their business. Their vans travel round cities and continually update their location on Twitter. Fans of the food outlet check when they are near and head out to meet them. Beyond the food, they've built a community of customers who love meeting up and sharing their comments through the site. Have a look: **twitter.com/ !/kogibbq/**.

Airlines like Lufthansa use Twitter and Facebook to update the status of their flights. Great if you're going to meet someone at the airport – you can find out exactly when the plane is arriving.

Crowd sourcing

The old-fashioned view of business is that you have to service customers and they pay you for your efforts. As new communication technologies appear, however, customer behaviour is changing. We don't want to be passive consumers any more. We want to be involved in shaping and making the product.

Many smart companies have harnessed this need for involvement by getting customers involved in voting for, designing and publicising products – all for free!

brilliant global example

South-African musician, Verity, struggled to get a recording contract. So she built on her fan base by getting them to buy her album – before she had recorded it. She did this by involving them in choosing which tracks would go on the album, what it would be called, cover artwork and so on. Fans loved the involvement, and over 2,000 people pre-ordered. That gave her the money to record it.

Public relations

Getting your face in the paper can be enormously satisfying (well, providing it was intentional). It makes you feel all-important for a while. It is cheaper than advertising (though don't forget to factor in your own time), and it's usually more believable than an advert.

Don't be afraid of journalists. They need stuff to fill their paper with so, if done well, you are doing them a favour.

brilliant tips

1 It must be compelling. If your news does not look eye-catching in the first five seconds, then it's unlikely to get you coverage.

2 Call first. I know it's more painful, but chatting to a journalist gives you a chance of selling your story.

3 Build up the human interest. They want to see a small business do well, particularly up against a big company.

4 If you've got a sympathetic contact, nurture them. Keep them posted with your good news, and if they run a good story – send them a bottle of wine as a thank you.

5 Try the picture desk as well. Sometimes an interesting photograph can get you coverage.

brilliant global example

A high-rise window cleaning company in Singapore hit on the ruse of dressing their staff in 'Spiderman' costumes. Soon, people would gather in the street to watch them, and it wasn't long before their photos appeared in a range of international newspapers.

Advertising

This is the first thing people think of in promotion. It's a sure-fire way to blow a lot of money very quickly. Make sure you've exhausted all the other avenues first.

- Remember AIDA? People need to hear your offer around four times before they take action. It's the same with advertising. Only advertise if you can afford to run at least four repeat adverts targeting the same audience.

- Make it different. Did I say that before? You don't have to spend a fortune.

- Don't be suckered in by convincing sales people who are offering you fantastic last-minute discounts. Bear in mind, if they think advertising is so effective, why are they using phone selling and not advertising to convince you?

- Look for unusual places to advertise (a man sold his forehead as advertising space on eBay for $30,000).

brilliant example

A leather coat store in Edinburgh had the sign: 'Due to an expensive divorce, Mr Toskana is having to sell his stock fast.' The cost of the sign must be a few pounds, but it is seen, and probably remembered, by thousands of people each day.

brilliant recap

While not a replacement for your sales effort, marketing can make your job easier. By now you should have:

- Ensured your brand is used consistently everywhere.
- Kept in touch with your existing customer base.
- Cross-sold other services to these customers.
- Built some simple referral mechanisms.
- Trialled direct marketing as part of a sales effort.
- Before building a website, thought what marketing purpose it's fulfilling.
- Used social media to reach a wider audience.
- Used PR only to support a sales effort.
- Ignored advertising unless you can afford to do it repeatedly as part of a campaign.

Epilogue

I hope by now your business is up and running. I hope you've not been put off by the bumps along the way (and not taken criticisms to heart), and taken time to celebrate the victories, however small they may be. Running your own business is a journey through time, and there are many seasons along the way. The most important thing is just to keep going.

I remember a tough period we went through in my business, one of those times when nothing you do seems to work. My co-director gave me the following extract. The tough times soon passed, and business picked up again, but the sentiments remain:

Until one is committed, there is hesitancy, the chance to draw back, always ineffectiveness. Concerning all acts of initiative (and creation), there is one elementary truth the ignorance of which kills countless ideas and splendid plans: that the moment one definitely commits oneself, then providence moves too. A whole stream of events issues from the decision, raising in one's favor all manner of unforseen incidents, meetings and material assistance, which no man could have dreamt would have come his way. I learned a deep respect for one of Goethe's couplets:

Whatever you can do or dream you can, begin it.

Boldness has genius, power and magic in it!

(W. H. Murray (1951) *The Scottish Himalayan Expedition*)

Useful contacts

Good business resources

Books

For motivation: *Think and Grow Rich*, by Napoleon Hill.

For systems: *The E-Myth*, by Michael Gerber.

For practical advice: *Inc. Magazine* **www.inc.com**.

For pitching: *Life's a Pitch...*, by Stephen Bayley and Roger Mavity; and *It's not how good you are, it's how good you want to be*, by Paul Arden.

Networking groups/websites

Startups: **www.startups.co.uk**.

Ecademy: **www.ecademy.com**.

Smarta: **www.smarta.com**.

Government support

The Business Links

There used to be a network of 45 local Business Links operating across England. These have been replaced by a call centre and online service. The Business Link website is still a comprehensive source of advice on funding, grants and legislation: **www.businesslink.gov.uk**.

Scottish Enterprise

In Scotland, the equivalent service is at **www.bgateway.com**.

HMRC

Her Majesty's Revenue and Customs is at **www.hmrc.gov.uk**.

UK Intellectual Property Office

Advice on patents and intellectual property is at **www.ipo.gov.uk**.

For young people

Prince's Trust and Prince's Scottish Youth Business Trust

Includes a directory of other young people starting in business, hints and tips at **www.princes-trust.org.uk** and **www.psybt.org.uk**.

Shell LiveWIRE

Help and advice for 16–30-year-olds setting up in business and runs a national business competition at **www.shell-livewire.org**.

Young Enterprise

A unique scheme to encourage and develop enterprise skills in students aged 4–25 at **www.young-enterprise.org.uk**.

For women

British Association of Women Entrepreneurs (BAWE)

This is a non-profit professional organisation for UK-based women business owners. Founded in 1953, BAWE encourages the personal development of member entrepreneurs and provides opportunities for them to expand their business at **www.bawe-uk.org**.

Business support groups

Federation of Small Businesses

The UK's leading lobbying and benefits group for small businesses. The website contains information concerning the key issues facing the small business sector today at **www.fsb.org.uk**.

Forum of Private Business

The Forum of Private Business (FPB) is a pressure group lobbying on behalf of members to change laws and policies for their future benefit. The forum also offers advice on problems such as red tape, employment law, health and safety and many other issues, at **www.fpb.org**.

Entrepreneurial Exchange

Run by entrepreneurs for entrepreneurs, the Exchange is Scotland's premier networking group for entrepreneurs (and now in London) at **www.entrepreneurial-exchange.co.uk**.

British Chambers of Commerce

The British Chambers of Commerce comprise a national network of Chambers, uniquely positioned at the heart of every business community in the UK, at **www.britishchambers.org.uk**.

Index

abilities, personal 7–8
accountants 103, 165–6
accounts
  abbreviated 102
  filing 102
  reconciliation 167
adding value 185
adventurous, becoming 26–7
advertising 26, 27, 209
  website 76–7, 204–5
  see also marketing
advice 53
  coach 50–2
  financial 173
  free 53
  mentor 54–8
agency theory 115
AIDA 115–16, 209
Air Miles 16
Allied Dunbar 140
Amazon 32
analysis of plan 65–6
  SWOT 97
Annual Accounting Scheme 172
Articles of Association 102
assets, building 7
auditing your skills 7–8

banks 88–90, 103
  and book-keeping 167
  checklist to support
      customers 91
  convincing them to lend 91–2
  small business banking 88–9
  traffic light system 89

benefits for customers 22–3
Benson & Hedges 42
BMW 202
Body Shop, The 85
Book People, The 21
book-keeping 8, 161–74
  hiring a book-keeper 167–8
  keeping records 166–7
bootstrapping 69–72
  techniques 70–2
branding 25–8, 198–200
  franchising 45–6
  selling your business 6
  value and premium brands 137
  web address 77
  see also marketing
Branson, Richard 43
bravery and risk 10
Bridge, Rachel 18
budget, personal survival 82
  see also finance
Buffet, Warren 200
business
  buying a 44–6
  franchising 45–6
  limited company 101–3
  partnership 52, 104–5
  selling your 6–7
  small business groups 51
  sole trader 103–4
  specialist 19
  see also advice; mojo
business angels 84–5
Business Growth Fund 93

business idea 34
  and change 16–17
  cultural variations 17
  giving away 33
  from hobby 18
  keeping quiet 33, 51, 58
  looking overseas 17
  and new legislation 16
  and new technology 17
  and new trends 16–17
  as problem solution 15–16
  protecting 30–3, 58, 177
  prototyping 40–2
  road testing 35–46
  supercharging 18–28
  see also road testing
Business Link 86, 87
business loan see finance
business name 28–9
business plan 63–6
  analysis 65–6
  funding 93–7
  layout of 96–7
  not perfecting 8
  see also pitching your plan
buying
  bootstrapping 69–72
  equipment 173
  see also purchases
buying a business 44–6
  caveat emptor 44
  franchising 45–6
  spinning out 44–5
Buytaert, Dries 33

Camelot 121
capital allowance 173
cash 157–61
  care of 168–9
  management 158–61
  see also finance
Cash Accounting scheme 172
cashflow 157

change
  becoming adventurous 26–7
  and ideas 16–17
Chegg 139
clients see customers
closing the sale 128
coach 50–2
  life coach 51
Cold Stone Creamery 22
commitment 10, 66
  and pitching your plan 95
Companies Act 102
Companies House
    paperwork 101–2
competition 22
  benefits of 40
  marketing 25–6
  price 140
  research 40
  working for 40
competitive advantage 32
competitors
  as mentors 56
  pricing 138, 139
  protecting your idea 33
concession in retail business 75
confidentiality
  clients' 20
  non-disclosure agreement 58
consistency and branding 199
contract, sales 129
copyright 30, 177
  posting to yourself 30, 177
corporation tax 102, 170
costings 64–5
  down time 65
  indirect costs 64
  your own time 64, 65
costs 186–7
  bootstrapping 69–73
  don't buy anything 70–1
  false economies 72–3
  franchising 45–6

getting deposits 71–2
reduction of start-up 67–78
shopping around 71
credit card financing 82, 89
credit crunch 90–2
credit, giving 159
cross-selling 201
banks 90
crowd sourcing 207–8
customers
   and banks 91
   benefits to 22–3, 25
   changing brand 27
   competition 40
   losing 141–2
   loyal 124, 179, 200–1
   managing expectations 151–2
   market research 42–3
   needs 15, 24, 28–9, 147
      and name of business 28–9
   niche business 20
   payment from 157
   pricing 141–3
   reassuring 198, 199
   retention 200–1
   selling to 120–30
   and social media 207–8

debtors 158
   Payment Chicken 160
debts, liability for 52, 101, 103,
      104
delegation 8, 188
delivery time 65
demand for product/service 124
deposits from customers 71–2
design, registering 30, 31
desire and passion 9
desk research 38–9
destination store 74
direct marketing 203–4
discounts, cash 169
distribution 119
domain names 31

down time 65
down-turn start-ups 90–1
Dragon's Den 84

e-commerce 27–8, 76–8, 204–6
   defensive moat 76
   service 77–8
e-mail newsletters 206
eBay 76, 150
Economist, The 31
employees see recruitment; staff
employers liability compulsory
      insurance (ELCI) 106
enterprise agency
      recruitment 188
Enterprise Department
      funding 86
Enterprise Finance Guarantee
      (EFG) 92–3
entertaining and tax 174
enthusiasm 9, 121–2
entrepreneurs, characteristics
      of 7–10
equipment, buying 173
European Investment Bank 93
experts 50, 52–7
   on tax 173
   using professionals 52–3

factoring 159
failure
   coping with 178–9
   fear of 10
   reasons for xi, 50
   support network 49–59
family, borrowing from 84
fear 10
Fear of Regret 198
features of products/
      services 22–5
Federation of Small Businesses
      (FSB) 53, 192
field research 39

finance 81–98
  banks 88–90, 91–2, 103
  bootstrapping 69–72
  borrowing 81, 82–3, 84
  business angels 84–5
  friends and family 84
  funding 92–7
  grants 86–7
  keeping the day job 83
  loans 87, 90
  overdrafts 82–3, 88–9
  personal guarantees 103, 178
  post credit crunch 90–2
  risks 10, 178
  savings 81–2, 89
  security 103
  soft loans 87
  working capital 81
  see also costs; pitching
financial projections 63–5, 94, 97
Flat Rate Scheme 171
Forms 10 and 12 102
franchising 45–6
free money myth 86
friends
  borrowing from 84
  not telling 51
  partnerships 52
fuel costs 173–4
funding 92–7
  alternative sources of 92–3
  pitching for 93–7
  plan 63, 93–4
  see also finance

gaps in the market 38
gender niche 20
generalists 19
giving up xii, 43
goals 9
Goldcorp 33
Google ad words 205
grants 86–8

handling fees 158
health and safety 105
health/living trends 16
Hilton-Barber, Miles 59
Hire a Hubby 20
hiring see recruitment
HMRC (Her Majesty's Revenue
    and Customs) 82, 103–4,
    105, 169, 171
home, working from 173
honeymoon period 37

ideas see business ideas
importing 149–50
  business ideas 17
initiative 9
Inland Revenue see tax
Innocent Drinks 41
innovation grants 86–7
inspiration 58–9
insurance 89, 105–7
  risks 178
  types of 106–7
  what to insure 106
Intellectual Property Office 30,
    31
interest rates 82
internet marketing 204–6
interviews
  pitching your plan 95–7
  recruiting staff 189–92
invoice discounting 159
invoices 160
isolation 50, 52

Jarron, Belinda 26
Job Centres 189
job descriptions 189–90
Joffe, Joel 140
John Lewis 104
journalists and PR 208

Karmi beer 20
key person insurance 106
KupiVIP 207

launching the business 113–79
Law of Unintended
        Consequences 41–2
lawyers 53–4, 177
leasing premises 75–6
legal action/letter to
        creditors 156, 157
legal employment issues 192
legal MOT 53, 173–4
legal requirements 101–7
legislation and ideas 16
letter of understanding 129
letters of intent and funding 94
Levi's 139
liability for debts 52, 101, 103,
        104
life coaches 51
limited company 101–3
loans *see* finance
locations 76–7
    see also property
loneliness 50, 52
loyalty schemes 200–1
Lütte Leihen 139

McCormack, Mark 69
McGlinn, Ian 85
Mailing Preference Service 203
market
    gap in 38
    ideas and 18
    niche 19–20
market research 38–43
    competition 40
    customers 42–3
    desk research 38–9
    field research 39
    prototype selling 40–1, 42
    useless methods 38–9

marketing 197–210
    approaches 203–6
    'burr of singularity' 27
    direct 203–4
    explosive 25–8
    online 204–6
    smoke and mirrors 198–9
    social media 206–8
    stunts 27–8
Memorandum of
        Association 102
mental preparation 114–18
mentor 54–7, 87
    business angels 85
    coach 50–2
    dos and don'ts 57
    preparation 56
    where to find 56
Mills, Keith 16
mistakes, admitting 179
mojo meter xii, 43, 49–50, 65
    coping with failures 178–9
    hitting brick walls 43
    inspiration 58–9
    justifying price 139–40
    paralysis by analysis 65–6
    party time 148
    reward yourself 119–20
    sacking someone 192–3
    time off 187–8
momentum, maintaining 66
money *see* finance
morale *see* mojo
motivation 9

name of business 28–9
    and customer need 28–9
    memorable 29
National Insurance (NI) 102,
        170
negotiation 129, 179
niche strategy 19–20, 25
non-disclosure agreement 58,
        177

objections, selling 123–5
objectives 6, 9
office, virtual 76
　see also premises
Ogilvy, David 27
online marketing 204–6
opportunities, business 16–17
opportunity cost of staff 186
outsourcing 186–7
over-trading 142
overdrafts 82–3, 88–9
overheads 141
overseas, ideas from 17
overseas suppliers 149–50
ownership of material, proof of 30

paperwork for starting up 101–2
Parker 25
partnerships 52, 104–5
　agreement 104
　with friends 52
　Scotland 52, 104
passing off 30
passion 9–10, 18
　and sales 118
patents 32
Payment Chicken 160
payments 158–61
　advance 158
　and tax 166
　see also cash
perfection 8
Perman, Ray 55
personal guarantee for funds 88
personality and skills 8
pitching your plan 93–7
　handling objections 95–6
　layout of plan 96–7
　revenue assumptions 94–5
　stress testing 95
plan *see* business plan
premises
　leasing 75–6
　paying less for 74–6
　sub-letting 73, 75

virtual 76–7
working from home 73–4
premiumisation of
　products 16–17
preparation 5–107
　for selling 114–18
Pret a Manger 199
price 25, 123, 124, 131–43
　be expensive 135, 136
　competitors 138, 140
　dos and don'ts 135
　increasing 141
　influences on 136–7
　justification 140
　losing customers 141–2
　negotiation 147
　problems with cheap 137–8
　and quality 138
　and service 77–8
Prince's Scottish Youth Business
　Trust, The 87–8
Prince's Trust 54, 76, 87–8
product/service 147–53
　3-stage exercise 23–5
　and business ideas 16
　design 21
　features and benefits 22–5
　patents 32
　price 131–43
　renting 139
　selling your business 6
　uniqueness 21–2
　and untapped needs 24
professional advice 52–4
professional indemnity
　insurance 107
profits 147, 157
　and tax 102–3
promotion 26, 197–210
　see also marketing
Proof of Concept 87
property
　retail 74–6
　as security 88, 103
　see also premises

protecting your idea 30–3, 58, 177
prototype 40–2
public liability insurance 107
public relations 208–9
publicity: and social relations 206–7
purchase ledger 167
purchases
  on behalf of customers 158
  claiming back 173–4
  recording 166

quality and price 138
questions
  at funding interview 95–7
  to ask suppliers 149
  when selling 122

receipts 166
recommendations 201–2
record keeping 166–7
recruitment 188–92
  agencies 189
  checking up 191
  finding staff 188–9
    free options 188–9
  interviewing 189–92
  online job boards 189
  sales persons 130
  see also staff
referrals, sales 123
rejection 114–15
  fear of 10
renting of products 139
research see market research
responsibilities at start-up 5
retail property 74–6
  as destination store 74
risks
  audit/check 177–9
  banks' view of 89
  becoming a risk taker 26–8
  financial 10, 178
  over-trading 142

road testing your idea 35–46
  asking competitors 40
  asking customers 40, 42–3
  Law of Unintended Consequences 41–2
  market research 38–43
  prototype 40–2
running a business 5–6, 181–210
  objectives 6, 9

sacking staff 192–3
Sainsbury's and Three Delta fund 9
sales/selling 113–31
  agency theory 115
  AIDA 115–16
  bonus 120
  closing 128
  cross and up-selling 200–2
  difficulties 114–15
  handling common objections 123–5
  hiring sales persons 130, 191
  hit rate 117
  importance of 113–14
  involving customers 122
  ledger 167
  losing 129–30
  negotiation 129
  passing gatekeepers 127
  preparation for 114–18
  price 131–43
  referrals 123
  rejection 114–15
  risks 178
  sales funnel 117–18, 178
  script 123
  techniques 121–30
  timing 115–16, 127
  using silence 129
  see also marketing
savings 81–2, 89
Scotland: partnerships 52, 104
search engine optimisation 76, 205

Seattle Coffee Company 17
self-confidence 139
self-employment 103–4
   and tax 170, 172
self-esteem 118–20
selling *see* sales/selling
selling your business 6–7
service 77–8, 147–53
   commitment 199–200
   prototyping 42
   see also product/service
Six Degrees of Separation 56
Seyssel, William 21
share issues 103
Shiny Kit Syndrome 71, 206
Slaters 75
small business banking 88–9
small business groups 51
Small Firms Loan Guarantee
      Scheme 92
small print 99–107
Smart, Ted 21
snog to slap ratio 116–17
social media 205, 206–8
   crowd sourcing 207–8
   customers 207–8
   publicity 206–7
soft loans 87
sole trader 103–4
sounding board 51
specialist business 19
spinning out 44–5
staff
   book-keeper 167–8
   checking 191
   employing 185–93
   entertaining 174
   interviewing 189–92
   national insurance 102
   non-disclosure agreement 177
   sacking 192–3
   sales person 130, 191
   when to employ 185–6
Starbucks 16, 17

strengths and weaknesses 7–8
stress 5
   see also mojo
subsistence, claiming for 173
success 49
   ingredients of 9
suppliers 143–52
   avoiding inertia 151
   challenging 148–9
   finding good 148–51
   getting the most from 148
   looking overseas 149–50
   manufacturers as 150
   non-disclosure agreement 177
   relationships 151
   terms 159
   wince at price 149
support network
   agencies 57
   building 47–59
   'dream team' 94
   inspiration 58–9
   mentor 54–7
   non-financial assistance 87
   other start-ups 51
SWOT analysis 97

Tait, Richard 119
target marketing,
      researching 38–43
tax 102–3, 169–74
   and cash payments 169
   credits 172
   HMRC 82, 103–4, 169, 171
      notifying 105
   limited company 101–3
   paying less 172–4
   rebate 82
   record-keeping for 167
   self assessment 104
   working from home 73
   see also book-keeping
Taylor, Paul 9
technology and business ideas 17

Three Delta fund 9
3G technology and texting 41
timesheets 185
Tom Hunter sportswear 75
trade marks 31, 177
training courses 87
travelling, claiming for 173
trends and ideas 16–17

unique product/service 21–2
up-selling 200

VAT 166, 167, 170–2
venture capital 86
virtual business 76–8

weaknesses, compensating
    for 7–8
website 76–7
    driving traffic to 76–7
    marketing 204–5
white elephant sites 39
WineSide 125
working capital 81
working from home 73

the brilliant series

Whatever your level, we'll get you to the next one.
It's all about you. Get ready to shine!

PEARSON